T0157488

DEEP INNER THOUGHTS

Concept Of Death, Overcoming Fear

Esther B. Jimenez

authorHOUSE®

AuthorHouse™
1663 Liberty Drive
Bloomington, IN 47403
www.authorhouse.com
Phone: 1 (800) 839-8640

Published by AuthorHouse 11/07/2015

ISBN: 978-1-5049-5567-6 (sc)
ISBN: 978-1-5049-5568-3 (e)

Print information available on the last page.

*Any people depicted in stock imagery provided by Thinkstock are models,
and such images are being used for illustrative purposes only.
Certain stock imagery © Thinkstock.*

This book is printed on acid-free paper.

Interior Designs and Cover Design by Esther B. Jimenez

*Because of the dynamic nature of the Internet, any web addresses or links contained in
this book may have changed since publication and may no longer be valid. The views
expressed in this work are solely those of the author and do not necessarily reflect the
views of the publisher, and the publisher hereby disclaims any responsibility for them.*

CONTENTS

MY INNER THOUGHTS PRAYER

O, my Almighty GOD, I bow down with humility, sincerely facing the reality of life, the life that I treasure so much, the life that You have entrusted in me.

Divine Creator, I can't thank You enough for this gift of life and all the blessings that I have received since birth. There are many things that I am thankful and grateful for, my LORD.

I am delighted to claim that I am created in Your Image and for being one of Your creations. In You I entrusted back my life LORD and I will wait until I receive Your final blessing which is the beginning of eternity.

I ask You LORD to grant me a safe journey when the time comes that You wanted me to be reunited with You and with my loved ones to the place called "HEAVEN" and this I pray in the name of the Heavenly Father, Amen!

DEDICATION

To our beloved deceased parents Honorata B. Jimenez and Pedro T. Jimenez, my uncle Severino T. Jimenez, my sister-in-law Arleen A. Jimenez, my first cousin Alexander B. Domingo, and a father like to me Jose M. Criste, and a mother like to me and Beth, Catalina G. Bernabe who had left us recently and to all our loved ones who have gone ahead of us, for the good memories they have implanted in our hearts. We miss them.

Not to forget, to all the souls in Purgatory. By dedicating this book to them is my way of praying for them.

PREFACE

I am here contemplating on the uncertainties of life…here in my own world in which my heart and mind are conversing with each other constantly. Recently, my mind and heart are battling with each other, whether to have a mammogram or not. I strongly felt the consensus of both. That is…I won't go for any diagnostic procedure. I am aware what the people around me will say and I could hear in my ears their voices saying "What's wrong with you? You're a nurse and you should know better".

I am also aware that some people will not understand my situation and some might understand and might be supportive. Rationalization aside, it is my strong discernment to just leave my breasts alone.

More than a month ago I was feeling the heaviness, the shooting and nagging pain at the circular part of my bilateral breasts. I felt the lumps on both. Breasts cysts or lumps scare most women because of the fear of being diagnosed with capital "c", cancer to be exact.

More than 2 decades ago, I used to submit myself for a mammogram and I did it for at least three times for the whole 2 decades and all of them with negative results. I stopped the yearly mammogram since then, (not aware of the reason why.) Often times, I was debating with the people who are breast cancer survivors. I hear from them the following comments or opinions.

"Early detection is better for early treatment."

"The percentage of survivors is higher with early detection than women who don't go for breast check-up and mammogram."

"Chemotherapy and radiation help diminish the size of the tumors."

"Remission rate is higher."

Indeed I am grateful for their concerns and I utmostly respect their opinions. Even the people who don't have cancer are encouraging me to do the annual mammogram. The ironic part is I am a nurse and as a nurse I should know better, right? Being a nurse or not being one has nothing to do with my inner thoughts.

Allow me to share with you a partial scenario of my life and please read in between the lines. I am requesting you to read in between the lines because I don't want to influence women to be cowards or to avoid seeing a specialist for women's physical problems. The sharing of my inner thoughts is to express my own insights, my desire to live **a quality life,** my coping mechanisms and most of all my strong faith in GOD and the prompts of the Holy Spirit. I would like to be a model in a positive way to women who are in the same situation as mine. I would like to share my insights.

I am enjoying my life now with all the gifts that GOD Has given me. Fear is out of the picture. I have beautiful and wonderful family and friends. They are all supportive of me, with my decision and everything that engulfs my situation.

Am I being morbid or am I being realistic?

I do not have to think that I have to leave this earth soon at a certain time because somebody says so.

At least nobody will tell me, "I am sorry you have this and that." or, "You only have three to twelve months to live." What a bomb shell!

The weatherman can forecast what the upcoming weather would be, but only GOD can forecast the time (our time) to leave this earth. He Has the final say.

You see, it's two different thing when a doctor tells a client "You have at least 3 to 4 months to live." Right there and then your outlook in life changes. Worries will kiss you. Fear will embrace you. But if you don't know the number of days, months or years you are to stay on earth, you can face death graciously through your spiritual preparation. Isn't it pleasant to think or even to imagine to live spiritually conscious and healthy as much as possible? If I have to die without knowing how soon it is, at least I can prepare myself without side thinking I have to go on with chemotherapy or radiation. Or worst case scenario, there will be no "time pressure."

That's it for being open and for being honest on how I feel and how I am going to deal with the uncertainties.

This is it…."My Deep Inner Thoughts…the Concept of Death… Overcoming Fear." Let's tackle it.

ACKNOWLEDGEMENTS

I would like to thank our Almighty GOD for giving us the wonderful gift of life and death as a blessing, for giving us the chance to stay on earth and fulfill His plans for us.

I thank You LORD for the gifts of the Holy Spirit and His prompts.

I would like to extend my sincere thanks to my deceased parents for giving me the inspiration…that is, pursuing my four books for publication. (This is in the year 2009-2010.) Even though they are no longer in this world, they still serve as my guidance through their goodness, kindness and unforgettable memories that they have implanted in me and of course in my family.

To my one and only sister, brothers, nephews, nieces, sister- in-laws, brother-in laws, grandchildren, great grandchildren, cousins and friends, for supporting me through their prayers despite of knowing the reasons why I am writing this book.

To Elizabeth P. Criste and Monalisa G. Bernabe thank you for believing in my deep inner thoughts, for helping me in reviewing my book, for their professionalism, honesty, loyalty and friendship.

To my deceased relatives, deceased friends, deceased Popes, nuns and priests, and all the souls in purgatory. Thank you for you are my foot rules in my journey to the Kingdom of GOD. I offer my prayers for you all.

To some funeral parlors and their staff especially the funeral directors whom I have encountered for their compassionate attitudes, their approachable manners and the kind services they have rendered to the family members and friends of the deceased. Knowing how they render the services due, I feel at ease thinking I would be treated with the same respect, compassion and gentleness when my time comes. Even at the last moment reassurance is at hand. I would like to special mention the Ahlgrim & Sons Funeral and Cremation Services, LTD for their excellent service in all aspects. With the experience we had recently having one of our loved ones serviced by them, we were amazed with smooth sailing of the family bereavement discernment. From the time we made the arrangement for the bereavement, we were already impressed the way the Funeral Director, Kathleen Ahlgrim handled the whole process. Thank you for making it light in our grief and sorrow.

And for all my true friends who stood by me with their dedication and laughter that bring joy into my life.

To Reverend Leon Rezula for his generous time that he devoted on reading my manuscript. Inspite of his busy schedule this summer like the church activities and his upcoming retirement, he managed to do the Foreword for my book. Thank you Father Leon for the heartfelt feedback of my manuscript. I wish for your happy, fruitful and blessed retirement.

Ultimately, to myself for the courageousness and honesty and for acknowledging that GOD loves me and so do I. Loving oneself brings out the Image of GOD in me as we are created in His Image. And for that, I should love myself. Two of the greatest commandments are " to love GOD above all and to love your neighbor as you love yourself." GOD loves us unconditionally with or without cancer and no matter what, He loves us with full support in everything we do.

MYSELF

Where are you myself? Myself, my being, my image ; I have to discover my true identity ; I am here in the midst of discovery ; Now I know the image I've grown ; Myself, I have found on my own ; I realized the truth behind myself; That… I am created in GOD's Image.

FOREWORD

Death is the Greatest Unknown…and the Fear of Death is the greatest fear of all. It is so very hard for us to imagine a time WHEN WE WILL NOT EXIST AS WE NOW DO… with comfortable and familiar surroundings, gathering with our families and friends. And it is impossible to know what death itself will be---because when it finally and fully claims each one of us-it denies us the voice which would share the experience with those who will follow us. Yes, death is the greatest unknown; and the fear of it prevents us from reflecting upon our Catholic Faith and sharing the Christian Hope that we all hold. The thought of death is not fair. There is a yearning inside of all of us, that once alive, *we should go on* –somehow-**forever!** And yes, that is part of GOD's plan! When we first learned the catechism, we encountered that "GOD made us to be happy with Him forever." We know that GOD's plan was frustrated by sin, which caused death to come into the world. GOD Himself would have to save us, and that happened actually by JESUS coming into the world, the Son of GOD, the innocent one, suffering and dying for **all** of our sakes. If GOD Is For Us, Who can be against us? He who did not spare His own Son but handed Him over for us all; how will He NOT give us everything else along with Him?" (Romans 8:38-39) St. Paul goes on to say, "I am convinced that neither death nor life, nor angels, nor principalities,nor present things, nor powers, nor height, nor depth, nor any creature—will be able to separate us from the Love of GOD that comes to us in CHRIST JESUS our LORD." The beloved disciple of the fourth Gospel also assures us: "Yes, GOD so loved the world that He gave His only Son, that whoever believes in Him may not die, but may have eternal life." (John 3:16)

Enter Estrella (Esther) B. Jimenez. She is a Filipino nurse who had worked in the United States. This helps account for her more Eastern influences on n confronting created reality, philosophy, art, faith, hope, love, Christian Living,-with Phenomenology, Existententialism, Personalism and Deep Spirituality. Her pattern of thought is that of the Mystic, really in the classic sense of that word. Esther is the Author of many articles and several books, including "365 Days Food For Thoughts","Bible Tidbits", and "What's In My Heart"—volumes I and II. This her newest work, "DEEP INNER THOUGHTS (Concept Of Death, Overcoming Fear)"—is truly an amalgam or a "pastiche" of Cosmology, Philosophy, Counseling Psychology and Spirituality. Esther confronted all of the issues I cited above in October, 2014, when a lump in her breast was discovered.She chose not to undergo the testing and not to have the mammogram. Confronted with the possibility of immanent death, she deeply reflected upon all this and wrote down her thoughts and prayers, impressions and insights. At this time, over and above all, she concluded that there can and should be first and foremost—firm trust in GOD and His Unconditional Love.

Yes, it's all here! The principles of our Catholic Faith, Bible, doctrine of Communion of Saints, Eucharistic Adoration, Detachment, Christian Suffering, the Immanence of GOD, Christian service and Stewardship, Prayer and how to pray,--with instructions in the classic age old prayer form of "Lectio Divina". All this poetically expressed and articulated and so beautifully inspirational! From" My Heartfelt Prayer',"Tell It Now, "The Power Of Forgiveness", "Focus On The Good Things", "GOD Is Enough","Never Doubt", "Time Is Gold","The Now","It's Never Too Late",'Attitude Of Gratitude",' A Desire To Serve","Compassion Prayer',My Inner Thoughts Prayer",--You get the idea. "The way I look at the world…" Esther says, "It is what you do with the time GOD is giving you. It is also the wisdom of knowing the will of GOD!"

Yes, indeed, after experiencing all the tenderness, the poetry, the artistry and wisdom of these deeply personal and shared inspirational reflections, we can truly echo the author's own concluding thoughts, that, indeed,…."GOD Is Enough","This fine work is truly…' A beautiful and Inspiring GIFT OF WISDOM"!!!

From the <u>Pastoral Constitution on the Church in the Modern World</u>—
of the Second Vatican Council:

We do not know the time when earth and humanity will reach their
completion, nor do we know the way in which the universe will be
transformed. The world as we see it, disfigured by sin, is passing away.
But we are assured that GOD is preparing a new dwelling place and
a new earth. In this new earth righteousness is to make its home, and
happiness will satisfy, and more than satisfy, all the yearnings for peace
that arise in human hearts. On that day, when death is conquered,
the sons of GOD will be raised up in CHRIST; what was sown as
something weak and perishable will be clothed in incorruption. Love
and the fruits of love will remain and the whole of creation, made by
GOD for man, will be set free from the frustration that enslaves it.

Reverend Leon J. Rezula (Retired) Pastor,

St. Julian Eymard Catholic Church, Elk Grove Village, Illinois

REVEREND LEON J. REZULA

Father Leon J. Rezula was ordained on May 14,1969.

Father Leon J. Rezula had served seven parishes as Associate Pastor in
Illinois. He was appointed as Pastor, back at St. Julian Eymard early
November 1999. Upon knowing this, he said, "I was grateful that I
had been here once before as associate pastor." "I am so deeply grateful
for the opportunity, I had to serve you here twice." "And also for the
friendships that I have made along the way. The Church is the People
of GOD, and the parishioners, the People, are the Church-not (just)
the building."

Reverend Rezula just retired a month ago and currently staying in his
newly purchased condo in Schaumburg- ten minutes away from St.
Julian, in case he needed to be there. He has served St. Julian Eymard
for almost 16 years.

ABOUT THE AUTHOR

Estrella "aka" Esther B. Jimenez, is a native of Manila, Philippines, a nurse by profession, a US Citizen and residing in Illinois.

She is a retiree now and spending her time painting on stones or rocks, sometimes on canvasses. She is joining different craft shows for her multiple rock painting exhibits from a pebble size to a garden size, from paper weights to garden display rocks.

She is a member of Authors Marketing Group of Illinois. She is also a member of Chicago Turtle Club. She loves pets and animals as evidenced by having adorable and beautiful orange-bellied turtles. One of them named Pong was trained by Esther to dance and walk with her. In tribute to Pong, there's a book about him written by her entitled "202 Turtle Haiku." Pong is eleven years old now still beautiful and adorable.

She just finished her training for the Breavement Ministry also known as Ministry of Consolation a month ago. And currently she's attending a 13th week support group known as " Grief Share". Esther is a people person. She loves to be with group who have common goals as hers.

She received the Editor's Choice Award in August 2004 and January 2008 presented by the International Library of Poetry. In June 2002 she was nominated as the Poet of the year by the International Society of Poets.

Whatever Esther does she prays for the guidance of the Holy Spirit and always relies on His power. And for her, the Holy Spirit is her Spiritual Director.

INTRODUCTION

Death is much, much equated to life in the manner that death exists only because life exists.

Life is…light
Death is…darkness

Death indeed happens…that is to give importance to life.

This book is not about how to cope with grief nor about dwelling on it. It is about my own facing of the uncertainty of death. The uniqueness of this book is that, it is a confession of an ordinary woman like me (actually this is my own confession), about pondering on how to face death gracefully and focusing on doing so without valid reason such as suffering from terminal illness of any sort. It is indeed just plain boldness on my part. It is a challenge not to fear death, but a challenge to love death as a friend, and to treat it as a blessing.

"Deep Inner Thoughts, Concept Of Death, Overcoming Fear" is the title I chose to express the whole meaning of conceptualizing, accepting and preparing myself to face the friendly welcomer, the final blessing of mankind called death.

My goals in this book are: to express my inner thoughts and feelings, to share my concept of death to the readers, to let the world know that there is a healthy way, a healthy approach to death.

As part of the title of the Book "Concept Of Death," it is a very broad phrase that threatens human beings in the midst of their normal life.

Death has different meanings to a lot of people-to the people in the convent, to the military group, to the people with criminal minds, to the people in the medical fields, to the patients in the hospital, to the elders in the Nursing Homes, to the ordinary ones like parents and children, and even to the animals and pets.

The following are some concepts of death. Some of them are my own concepts.

that...Death exists when life exits. If there is no life, there is no death. Death is not the end of life, it is the beginning of knowing its essence.

that...Death is a good-bye; Birth is a welcome.

that...Death comes unannounced, that life comes announced.

that...Death is the expiration date of the life's promotion.

that...Death is cold, life is warm

that...Death is breathless, life is breathing alive.

that...Death is holy, a part of the gift of life

that...Death gives birth to eternal life

that...Death is direct holy conveyor to Heaven

that...Death is the end of earthly life

that...Death is the birthday of the soul into Heaven

that...Death is rest in peace

that...Death is a relief

So let us glorify GOD in life and in death.

Death has always been the greatest of mysteries. I haven't experienced death. I've read that experience of death is as individual as the experience of life. We can only theorize, read, and of course pray on how death actually occurs, but we will never know what it truly is until we experience it ourselves. There are books that tackle the near-death experience and the common things experienced in the near-death situation and such are: going through a tunnel, or meeting a loved one, or seeing a bright light, or encountering a spiritual being, or they are tired and exhausted. Inspite of those experiences, at the end they feel the peacefulness.

There are more meanings, definitions or concepts of death. You might have your own definition but the bottom line is, it is about the how to face death? And what to do to befriend it and the consequences to consider to fulfill this friendship. Remember to invest good deeds on earth, and always implant this into your heart, "that JESUS is LORD".

Ultimately, this book is to acknowledge GOD's way of helping the mankind to cope with the fear of the unknown and the known and to let us know that death is part of His plan. GOD's plan is a life cycle, which is from womb to tomb.

CHAPTER I

Fear Of Dying

I do not have a survey percentage of the number of people who are scared to die or what is called,"thanatophobia." Yes, "thanatophobia" means the fear of dying. I haven't encountered anyone yet who is not scared to die. When asked why they're scared to die, these are some of their responses-

"I still have a lot of things to do"
"I am not ready yet"
"I still want to see the world around"
"I'm still young to die"
"I can't afford to die, I am the bread winner."
"I want to get married and have a family"
"I have a strong phobia of dying"

Why are we so afraid of death? The answer is simple. It is an unknown experience. A lot of people are not comfortable to talk about death. The only people that are bold enough to express what death is, are the ones who have gone through what is called "a near-death" experience and shared their experiences of what it is like, to die.

I'm sure there are many more responses out there and many can relate to these responses. I think the fear of dying has something to do with the concept of death. I would like to share three more concepts of death and real stories behind. From these stories you will be able to grasp how people are different in handling their fear or non-fear of death.

The other night I was watching a television series program and there was this guy who was in a death row. He was scheduled for a lethal injection as

1

his death penalty. Looking at his face I could see how anxious he was. He looked so nervous and he was so restless. Evidently he didn't want to die. Just imagine in few seconds it will be the end of his life.

I am mentioning this type or this way to die because this is one of the concepts of death. It seems like this is one unwanted death by the sentenced inmate. And yet this kind of death is the one that the victim's relatives are awaiting for, through the glass panel of the death chamber. All of them wanted to see this inmate dead after the lethal injection was administered. In this scenario, death is wanted and unwanted. In our country, death penalty has been abolished. Death was then a subject of choice by the judicial system. Death is a major part of living in this earth.

This is not a debate between a capital punishment nor a life sentence. This is about the power of death in which GOD is the only judge and can only judge. Whatever the cause of death, may it be natural or intentional, the bottom line is, be prepared and be ready to face the Almighty.

I have mentioned in the early part of this book that if there are zillions of people die every year, there are also zillions of causes of death…but there are only few concepts of death. There are natural death, death from accidents, mercy killing death, death from suicides and shoot to kill death. What I meant by shoot to kill death is not the shooting in the war, nor the shooting of villains like in a movie, and not even the sniper shooting. What I meant is a hit man who is being paid to kill someone or an assassin intending to kill the target person.

About four decades ago, my uncle had an encounter with a member of a gang. He was threatened by that gang member to kill him. My uncle was shot and he was already dead on arrival when the ambulance reached the emergency room. This is the kind of death that I feel is unfair. It could not be GOD's will, but still GOD took care of the bereaved. GOD was with us all the time. This is another concept of death, even though it is unpsychological. Whatever my concept of death is, I now learned to embrace death as a way of exiting the earth with a holy plan and a chance to go to the heavenly place.

What do euthanasia and mercy killing have in common aside from their meaning being similar? Both of these words has a strong connotation of death. Let's see the whole definition of euthanasia. According to Mr. Webster, it is a Greek word which means "eu" easy, "thanatos" death. So it is "easy death." Euthanasia is the practice or act of intentionally ending a life of an individual who is hopelessly sick or injured for reasons of mercy. Mercy killing is the act of putting to death painlessly or allowing a person to die, as withholding medical measures from a person or animal suffering from an incurable especially a painful disease. There is another term that we need to be aware of... that is "assisted dying". It is when a terminally ill, mentally competent adult, making the choice of her/his own free will and after meeting strict legal safeguards, take prescribed medication which will end her/his life. Euthanasia, mercy killing or assisted dying is a very controversial and sensitive issue. One of the issues is a question that always come up like," Are you in favor of euthanasia or mercy killing?"We are not going to get the consensus here. But if I am asked of such question, my answer is "no".

I know of somebody who was diagnosed with cancer of the lungs stage IV and had chemotherapy. He was in severe, agonizing and unbearable pain. He asked his girlfriend and mother for euthanasia and begged for mercy killing. They were against his wishes. When his girlfriend asked him to pray with her, he seemed irritated because he was in his agony of pain. His skin was so sensitive. His mother can't even hug him. This was a heart breaking scene. This is what I am talking about, agonizing and unbearable pain. And if somebody is in this kind of situation, the quality of prayer is lost. The severe discomfort steals the quality of prayer. Instead of focusing on prayer, the attention is focused on self.

It is not only the people with suicidal ideation who are not scared to die. Patients with terminal illness with unbearable pain would also express the desire to die. I do not condemn those people who wish to die through mercy killing. I respect them and their wishes.

3

*Again, I can't emphasize enough my desire to have **a quality life** in the midst of my heavy feeling. All I can say is, prayer is so powerful and I pray for every patient who wishes for mercy killing. May they feel the Presence of GOD and I pray to our LORD to make them feel His Presence. I noticed that the concept of death in this situation is different. Death for them is a"relief". In their minds euthanasia or mercy killing is an easy way out of the misery. This is a unique concept of death.*

Thanatophobic people will say anything just to avoid encountering the mysterious death. Sometimes we need to change our concept of death in order for us not to be scared.

Let me share with you a beautiful poem about death. Read the "Music of Silence" here in this Chapter. It gives a different meaning of death and I would like you to feel the essence of it. The more I am acquainted with death, the more I feel at ease with my present physical discomfort.

As I've been mentioning about the people who are afraid to die, I just heard a priest's sermon about dying. He confessed that he is also scared to die and he was trying to overcome his fear. Some people don't even want to talk about it. Even my own mother, didn't want to die yet because she wanted to witness her grandchildren of their growing up.

My sister-in-law who was given nine months to live after she was diagnosed with lung cancer was bold enough and had strong will to live. She would like to attend and to witness her son's college graduation, in two year's time. Unfortunately she didn't make it that long. She had lived for at least two years after she was diagnosed of having lung cancer.

My aunt was struggling and even shouting when she was on her death bed uttering,"I don't want to die, please help me."Bless her heart, she died in vain not in peace. I believed that she has peace now through all our prayers in every mass all over the world. We should remember that praying for the souls is part of the mass service. It is universal.

How about the people who were victims of airplane crash or the 911 event? What was going on in their minds few seconds or minutes before they die? Have you ever thought of putting yourselves in their places and maybe in your imagination? I bet you would be scared too.

Don't you know that Paul and the other great Christians were not afraid of death?, They faced death confidently, squarely and courageously. They knew that CHRIST promised eternal life for those who believed in Him, as in *Philippians 1:21, it says "For to me, living is CHRIST and dying is gain."*

How about myself? Am I thanatophobic? Am I scared to die? Well, few years ago I used to be very scared just to think I would be six feet under. Indeed just the thought of it scared me. Lately, a lot of things is going on in my mind. I strongly feel I need to prepare for the uncertainty of death.

Again, I still feel the heaviness and pain on both breasts. The cysts are still there. The pain is on and off. For many years now, I have changed my attitude towards submitting myself for a mammogram. I will explain to the best of my ability why I am adamant not to have breast examination. I feel that after I have explained my reasons, you would create in your mind your own opinions. So, I'll relay everything as a story- telling…

I am enjoying my life now. I am a retired nurse but don't be surprised if I tell you that I don't have enough means for my extra spending. I'm on my disability pay every month. I live with my cousin who is also a nurse. I am not ashamed of what my life had been because whatever I did and wherever I was, are still part of me. So, let's go direct to the point. I didn't have a smooth employment history because I was suffering from depression and diagnosed to have one a decade ago. I was under Prozac and I had it for eight months only, had my regular one-on-one session with a psychologist and a psychiatrist. I tried to cope and tried to reach out to my loved ones. I had a very supportive family and my spirituality became stronger. I could say I am a depression survivor. During that time, I learned to use a paint brush dipped it on a paint and started smearing the canvass.

I didn't realize that I have the gift of art. At present time I am not buying canvasses anymore. I am picking-up stones/rocks of different sizes and shapes to paint and create figures of animals such as (elephants, turtles, owls, dogs, cats, fishes, chicks, snakes, pandas, monkeys, beetles and many more), flowers and fruits and even Santa Claus figures and Blessed Virgin Mary's images and more. There's delight in my heart doing this art work.It is therapeutic for me and aids me in coping with my stress.

As I've been mentioning, I was able to write books and this again helped me in my coping. I thank the Holy Spirit for letting me unwrap my gifts. My coping mechanisms are very effective. Part of my coping mechanisms is, learning to focus my thoughts into positive things. My spirituality became stronger especially when I started to join a Catholic charismatic group. My relationship with the Almighty aided me in my spiritual healing.

As you could see this life is very simple and that's my life. Now if in the middle of this simple, enjoyable and stress free life an unpleasant news arrived, then everything will change. If I would go and see a doctor and go through all these oncologic, diagnostic procedures and I hear I have a cancer, then this will be the end of my simple life. No matter what I say, whatever my reasons are for my hesitancy to have a mammogram, there will still be a lot of condemnations I would be hearing here and there. One of the comments again would be, "She doesn't know what she's saying nor doing."

One question that has been asked by many is, "How would you know if you have cancer or not, if you don't want to have breast exam, mammogram or biopsy?"I am going to welcome this question graciously and with humility by strongly giving my reply," If you're with GOD, who could be against us? It's a legit question. It's true, how sure am I that what I am physically feeling would lead to cancer? Or not at all.

Only GOD knows the answer to everything. I am relying only on GOD's healing power and the power of the mighty deeds. I claimed His power that is already in my life. This GOD's power is my only weapon for my holy discernment…and one crucial decision is about my mammogram.

If the result would be positive, I won't go for any breast surgery nor any invasive treatment. I want to have **a quality life.** Had it been my fate to be diagnosed with breast cancer, my life would totally change. The **quality of my life** would be diminished because I would be preoccupied with that positive result, (that is having cancer.) Aside from the healing power that I am relying on, I learned to replace my fear with faith. My faith of living with GOD cannot be broken. I am inspired with one of the Bible verses, as in *Romans 14:8, which says, " If we live, we live to the LORD, so whether we live or die we belong to the LORD."* What a great feeling knowing that GOD owns us.

My fear of dying is now replaced with my faith in living and for me I am still looking forward to attain the final blessing gracefully. The following poem is an excerpt from my book, "What's In My Heart? Vol. II, which is about the things that might be in someone's mind few seconds to death.

THE LASTS OF THE LAST

What could it be in a person's mind at the verge
of the approaching death?
I like to get into their minds now;
And these I heard:
"I'm prepared"
"I don't care"
"I wish to live longer"
"Where will I go"

"I don't want to go to hell"
"Is there a purgatory?"
"Heaven would be wonderful"
"Thank You LORD for my transformation"
"I just wish I made the difference"
"I will miss my loved ones"
"GOD please forgive me"
"I don't deserve this"
"Thank You, I am ready"
"Will you give me another chance?"
"Enough is enough"
"Pain is unbearable"
"Pain is worthy of my sacrifice"
"I know I will be with our Creator very soon"
"Last thought, I thought"
"Last wishes, I wish"
"Last request, granted"
"Last rites, rites of penance and
reconciliation"
"Last moments, moments of truth"
"Last time, zero hour"
"Last person, myself"
The Last of everything is GOD"s Infinity.

You can add your last wishes or last thoughts if you want.

The final words of a dying person are precious to those left behind. Nothing is important to a dying person except to ask for forgiveness and to have a holy closure with their love ones. For me, the most heart-breaking last words are the seven last words of our LORD JESUS when he was on the cross. They are the best words that we can use for pondering and for meditation. The core message here is surrendering our everything to GOD.

I have mentioned that I've never known anyone who aren't scared to die. I would like to apologize for not remembering that there are people who aren't scared to die. These are the ones who are victims of suicidal ideation. Either they are not aware of what they're planning to do (like killing themselves) because they're under medication, or they are drug addicts who maybe lost their insights to live due to severe depression.

As I mentioned earlier another beautiful creations who are not scared to die are those finding ultimate relief from their agony of pain, the ones asking for mercy killing.

In "Heaven Is For Real", the book that I just read, the character named Colton is not scared to die because he had seen Heaven. He had so much to say about his experience in Heaven. For him it is a delightful feeling to see Heaven again and death is not a threat at all.

Let us not allow our fear to empower us about leaving this world. Death is a Friendly Welcomer, isn't it? Here is a poem that might change ones concept of death and might help us welcome death as a friendly welcomer.

THE MUSIC OF SILENCE

I can hear the rhythm of a voice in my heart
The sound of stillness rings in my ear
I need to play the music and need to listen
As my heart desires
But only Him our GOD who can understand
The Music of Silence.
Moments come and go
I ponder the thoughts of how to let myself
Express the uncertainties
Doubts and sureties shake hands together,
Letting the truth come out
Fear of the unknown and known
The mystery of leaving this wonderful earth

The reality of vanishing the scary thought of
the slowly approach, and the one thing
Sure to happen soon, or what seemed to
Presume as "later,"
Can't even mention the word…
Now I can say, "death" is just around the corner
Waiting, not rushing but patiently waiting
I even hear of known people who just bid
Good-byes, some sudden and some
Suffered with terminal illness.
It is okay to talk about death, because
That is part of living, knowing that life is a
Temporary thing.
We have a Great Father who created us and
Allowed us to feel and experience how it is
to have a life…
that everything is in His Hands,
the Eternal Plan is His, the Almighty One.
Can I call you a Friendly Welcomer,
Instead of death?
Are you the Music Of Silence?

I learned not to be scared to die when my parents died. It taught me to face the reality of death. It gave me hope that someday, my parents would be there waiting for me in Heaven. Shall I say I came to master the death concept?

I wrote the following poem when my mother died and after eleven months my father passed away, too.

MASTERING DEATH CONCEPT

I sympathize with the grievers, losing someone they loved
I extend my condolences by any means
I experienced to lose someone a relative, an aunt, an uncle,
a cousin, a grandma and a grandpa and a best friend.
It pained me to think they were gone,
Oblivion from the earth.
But…I have never been in someone's shoes, losing
a mother, until last year of November, wherein I
celebrated my 62nd birthday at the funeral home,
where we also had a vigil for my mother.
She was breathless, cold, stiff lying peacefully
On a beautiful casket.
We could still see her lovely face with traces
Of beauty from her youthful days.
Yes, that was painful, hurting and nerve-breaking
knowing that my mother would soon be gone
out of sight, our beloved mother bound to Heaven
to join the angels and saints.
We really have to die before we can see the
Kingdom of GOD, it's the reality of life and death.
With the near- death experience my mother had,
she was able to reconcile with our LORD, and
seeing our Blessed Mother in her short journey,
I know she died in a state of grace.
Death is not the end of life, it is the beginning of
knowing its essence.

With this mastering death concept, my fear of dying is
gone. Another poem that inspired me to write is entitled,
"In A State Of Grace"
Actually, I have a poem written in the next few pages entitled,
"A Preparatory Prayer". It is somewhat related to this poem.

In A State Of Grace

We don't hold the time, we can't tell when
We know it will come, but are we in a state of grace?
Every time I pray I ask our Almighty, to grant my
Family the grace of sweet forgiveness,
In the hour of death,
Recently, exactly a month ago, our beloved
Mother was called by our Creator and we
Witnessed her journey and how she went through
Was she in a state of grace?
Was she ready to leave the earth?
Did she know she was called home?
Yes, and she tried to let us know.
She claimed of being with the three people
One of them was our Beloved Mother, our
Blessed Virgin Mother, who asked her if she
was ready? When she nodded her head, she
was asked to go back, to talk to three relatives and
to tell them to let her go so she can be with her in
the final journey.
When she came back from coma, she asked my two
brothers and my nephew to let her go and to pray
for her so she could be with our Blessed Mother,
in her final adieu.
In as much as it hurts, to let go of our mother,
we have to give her up and surrender everything
to GOD, for He will take care of her in Heaven.
LORD, thank You for a peaceful death that You
have granted our mother.
There was a delight in our hearts to know
that she is in a state of grace.
We pray for her eternal rest in peace

And to continue the perpetual light
To shine upon her and may she be in Your
Kingdom, now and forever, in JESUS name
We humbly pray, Amen!

After this heartfelt message, I would like to confirm that
If you are with GOD who could be against us?
Before we leave this chapter,"Fear Of Dying," I thought of
creating a formula for fear of dying, that is… In A State Of
Grace Plus Reassurance Of Heaven, multiply by Faith,
Equals I am Ready...(to face the Music of Silence)

CHAPTER II

Prayers

Liturgical Mass is the highest form of prayer. So, when you attend the Sunday Mass or any day mass, it is a complete recipe of prayers. At the start of the mass is a prayer already. Every part of the mass is a prayer or a form of prayer. The essence of petition, consecration and offering is praying for the souls in purgatory, prayers for our loved ones who have gone ahead of us.

Every time I feel the heaviness and pain on my breasts, I pray right away and I offer my discomfort to GOD our Refuge. Prayers have big role in my decision. I have the Holy Spirit to aid me in this crucial discernment. That's why you are reading my book now, because that is the strong prompt of the Holy Spirit for me to share, express and write my deep inner thoughts about it.

In my life today, I rely very much on the power of prayers. If my life was like my life before, I won't be able to survive this crisis. I would be struggling with overcoming my fears. I fervently pray for everything. I learned to offer everything to our LORD and I always ask for the guidance of our generous Advocate, (the Holy Spirit). I gain my spirituality mostly during my adoration (spending time in front of the Blessed Sacrament to pray and meditate.) I always try to have my personal prayer time. From the time my life was transformed, I find myself contented, found solace and peace in my everyday endeavor. One of the constructive things that happened during my transformation was I wrote a lot of inspirational poems. Let me share with you two of my poems, excerpts from my book "What's In My Heart? Vol. I"

One of the prayers that I wrote is entitled "My Heartfelt Prayer" as follows-

MY HEARTFELT PRAYER

O LORD GOD, how awesome You are
And how great and wonderful as ever
I can't thank You enough for all the
blessings and graces that we receive
everyday of our lives.
At times I feel unworthy of Your
love and mercy, but You let me feel
that nothing and nobody can distract
the relationship I have with You.
The feeling of unworthiness is washed away.
And You are replacing it with Your
love and care
O LORD Almighty, the great Healer of all
make me humble and make me aware that
You are always there
Grant me O LORD the Holy virtues I needed
to use as my weapon in this material world
And constantly touch my heart and mind
To let me feel Your Presence all the time
I pray my LORD, in JESUS name, Amen!

I would like to continue sharing my prayers.
I hope you can relate with the following
inspirational insights-

MY DAILY GOSPEL

I will feed my mind with positive thoughts
I will feed my heart with gratitude

I will feed my soul with pure intention
I will feed my eyes with the beauty of nature
I will feed my ears with the sounds of Psalms
I will feed my faculties with the radiant power
The power that connects to our Creator
I will feed my being with holiness and wholeness
Yes my LORD, I will feed myself with the peace in
my heart for the glory of my One and Only GOD.

Prayer is a time spent in the presence of GOD, a way to commune with Him. In prayer there is delight, peace and joy. Whatever you pour out in silence, GOD is there to listen. Just remember that our LORD JESUS is just a prayer away. I would like to share some of my personal prayers.

I suggest that every time you pray or think of talking to GOD, have a pen and paper with you or maybe a journal book. Writing to GOD is a way to release your heartaches and any emotional tensions. Writing your inner thoughts eases your burden, the burden of pain and suffering. Anything that your heart says is already a prayer, especially when you talk to GOD.

Part of my longing for complete healing or even a partial one is writing psalms of my own. So I have this poem written entitled "My Psalms For You LORD".

My Psalms For You LORD

My soul thirsts for You,
my heart speaks of You
O LORD my most Redeemer;
I humbly bow down
With my knees on the ground
O LORD, the Forgiving One;

Your name I exalt
Your words I revere
My LORD thank You for Your Son;
I praise and worship You
With profound reverence
In the silence of my heart
I feel Your Presence;
I pray for peace and harmony
For the entirety
I shout for joy and delight
I lift up my soul
You are my Protector;
I surrender my everything to You
I ask for forgiveness of all my sins
To You I thank for all the things
I have received
And to You I am returning my soul
And my Being,
For You are my Divine Creator and Savior!
Alleluia! Amen!

Prayer is indeed powerful. GOD listens to every prayer and answers as well. He won't say no to any prayer. He would only delay the answer, for there's always a reason behind everything. He would give us wisdom and insight to let us know why our request prayer was not answered yet. We can pray anytime and anywhere, but it is still essential to have a personal prayer time. In personal praying, you would be able to know our LORD more and would have a more intimate relationship with Him. Experience for yourself how it is to have a personal prayer time.

Personal Prayer Time

Alone with GOD is what it is,
talking from the heart is what it takes,
to listen attentively, to meditate on

His Word O Holy Spirit come in our midst.
Allow me LORD to commune with You
To pour out all my concerns
To praise, honor and exalt Your name
To Thank You my LORD for everything.
Guide me O LORD in my prayer time
To be sincere and not just to mime
To spend sometime to feel Your Presence
To ponder on GOD's Word O Holy Triune
LORD JESUS I need You in my life
I crave and long for Your warmth and love
I ask You my LORD for mercy and grace
For a gift of personal prayer and a
deep relationship
Yes LORD, prayer is my way of life
Personal prayer time my sincere desire
Let me be worthy of Your Kingdom
And let your forgiveness be at hand
All this I pray in Holy Triune's name, Amen!

In time of distress and desperation we beg our GOD to help us.

We are just the humble hungry souls that needed to be fed spiritually. Let's read a prayer of the hungry soul.

THE PRAYER OF THE HUNGRY SOUL

I crave for the consoling words from a high Spirited soul
I thirst for the water from the Holy Quencher
I seek for the power of the inner healing
I clenched my fist from the aching pains
O LORD, the Father of mercy look into the heart
Of your grieving child,
I grieve for the loss of my identity
I searched for myself's dignity
I long for your touch and warm embrace
I surrender myself and my all
Please lift me up from the agony of sins,
My hungry soul I give in
O LORD, my GOD, my plea I beg of you
To listen and grant me the peace I need
Here, now and forever, Amen!

I have written a lot of prayers for different professions, people, occasions, events, and certain individuals. The prayers that I selected here are as important as in all my prayers. There is one prayer I wrote that pertains to this book itself, and this is one of my deep inner thoughts. The following is one of my utmost prayers here on earth and my wish before I reach the final blessing.

A PREPARATORY PRAYER

LORD GOD, I humbly bow down to You
To offer all my concerns, many a few
To ask for forgiveness and mercy O LORD
To be a forgiving person, too.

I have a lot of asking to do my LORD
But I have to thank You first, that I should do
Yes LORD, I am nothing without You
And I surrender everything to You
Whatever I think, say and do
From my heart I speak and that LORD
You already know
LORD, the thing that concerns me most
is the request of mine to ask You to grant
pardon of our sins (my sins and the sins
of my family and loved ones) and grant
us a good preparation, as in State of Grace,
I pray this in JESUS name, Amen.
One of my wishes before I vanish from this earth
is to die in a state of grace, (me, my family and
my loved ones.) I knew in my heart my parents did
have a holy closure with You, my Almighty.

I would like to conclude this chapter of Prayer with another prayer…

The A B C… of How To Pray.

Pray with Adoration…I worship and honor You LORD with profound reverence and I magnify Your name.

Pray with Benevolence … I bow down to You with my knees on the ground to show You my utmost reverence and profound respect.

Pray with Contrition…LORD, I ask for Your love and mercy, for Your constant forgiveness, for all of my sins and wrong doings and the things I failed to do as a true Christian.

Pray with Divinity…LORD, I pray for holiness in my life. I offer to You my humanity that I may be divine in my ways.

Pray with <u>Exaltation</u>…I exalt Your name and glorify You through my songs and my playing guitar, tuning with the Christian worship songs.

Pray with <u>Faith</u>…I surrender everything to You my LORD, without any doubt, and that You may hear and listen to my hungry soul. I know it from my heart that You'll guide me always.

Pray with <u>Gratitude</u>…I thank You for everything my LORD, for the gifts of the Holy Spirit and the gift of life.

Pray with <u>Humility</u>…LORD, I know that I can't do anything without You. I am a sinner and I needed Your grace and I needed to be more repentant.

Pray with <u>Intercession</u>…I pray for all the souls in Purgatory, for the people who are asking to pray for them and for those who have no one to pray for them. And I ask for the help of the Queen of Intercessor, our Blessed Mother Mary to pray with us and for us.

Pray with <u>Joy</u>…LORD, there is delight in my heart knowing You are there to guide me all the time. We rejoice Your Presence.

Pray with <u>Kindness</u>…LORD, grant me the gift of Random Act of Kindness that I may be able to extend my help to others, including pets and animals and even to strangers.

Pray with <u>Love</u>…LORD, love is a powerful tool to any relationship. I am blessed with the love of family and friends. Thank You my LORD for Your unconditional love and the love of Your Son, JESUS.

Pray with <u>Meditation</u>…I always crave for my conversation with You LORD. I always feel Your utmost Presence when I meditate. Meditating on Your Word is so powerful. LORD grant me moments of solitude with You.

Pray with <u>Never-ending Prayers</u>…LORD, few times the phrase "unceasing prayers" are mentioned in the Bible. Yes, it is essential to pray unceasingly because it is our way of life.

Pray with Obedience... LORD, I pray to be more obedient with my undertakings like Your Holy Ten Commandments. May You grant me the gift of fasting on Lent seasons and help me in my thoughts of justification. I honor our Blessed Mother Mary for her utmost obedience.

Pray with Praise... LORD to praise You is to honor You and worship You with our utmost reverence. We profoundly acclaim Your kindness, greatness and goodness. I praise You for everything with my humble gratitude.

Pray with Quest...LORD my Holy Quest is to know You more and to have a holy intimate relationship with You. I pray LORD to be more holy and be more repentant and I needed Your grace to fulfill that.

Pray with Reverence...LORD, I thank You for the gift of prayer. A prayer without reverence is not as effective as with reverence. I pray for the gifts of the Holy Spirit to be more reverend.

Pray with Supplication...LORD, thank You for answering our prayers. Again, *the Holy Bible says, "Ask and you shall receive".* I earnestly and humbly ask for Your love and mercy. Let us feel Your Presence wherever we are and whatever we do.

Pray with Thanksgiving... LORD, together with our unceasing prayers are our unceasing gratitude for everything. I thank You for the gift of life, the gift of family, the gift of friends and the gift of community. Most of all, I thank You for the gifts of the Holy Spirit.

Pray with Understanding...LORD, You are the most understanding of all, in this world that You created. I pray for the gift of understanding, that I may think of others first before I think of myself and to love them unconditionally.

Pray with Virtues... LORD, praying with virtues needed Your grace. I pray that You may grant me virtues to use in dealing with my daily endeavors. Help us cultivate more virtues for a better relationship with one another.

Pray with <u>Willingness</u>…LORD, You have granted us the freedom to pray, and we have to have willingness of heart to pour out our concerns. I thank You for allowing me to surrender my being to You and have the willingness to let You know I give in to Your power over me.

Pray with <u>X-citement</u>…LORD, there is delight and joy in my heart whenever I am at the chapel or church especially in front of the Blessed Sacrament I know that excitement is not jumping for joy, but heart pounding for Your Presence. I thank You my LORD for the reason to be joyful with Your utmost Presence.

Pray with <u>Yearning</u>…LORD, I am hungry for Your Word. I always look forward to have a conversation with You. I yearn for Your love and mercy. Thank You for Your Presence.

Pray with <u>Zeal</u>…LORD JESUS, I pray that You will grant me more spiritual tenacity so I can be of service to You. I love to serve You with zealousness, with my fervent prayers.

Praying is already part of my life. Without prayer, my life is a mess. I am most thankful that in this stage of my life I am given the chance to center my life in prayer. I am getting my strength from GOD through my fervent prayers. O LORD Almighty, thank You for the gift of prayer.

PRAYER FOR THE DEAD

Almighty Father GOD, look down in pity and
compassion on the souls of our dear dead.
Let Thy perpetual light shine upon them,
forgive all their sins and grant us the joy of
reunion in everlasting bliss.
May their souls and souls of all the faithful
departed, through the Mercy of GOD, rest
in peace, Amen!

CHAPTER III

Eulogy

When someone dies, it is a customary in most cases to give a "eulogy," that is honoring the person during the funeral service. Too bad the person can't hear those honoring words given by his/her friends and loved ones anymore. Can we honor someone that can reciprocate to say "thank you " for the honoring words?

The reason why I included Eulogy as one of the chapters is to be aware that honoring or saying something good to someone should be cultivated as a good virtue. Eulogy is always correlated with death, with funeral service and usually speaking in front of a casket or coffin and with the listening people called mourners. For some people, eulogy strikes them as a scary scene, because you would be talking to someone so quiet, breathless, cold and lying on a coffin.

We can re-enact the eulogy scene by communicating with each other. It could be between husband and wife, mother and daughter, brother and sister, friend to friend, and any couple dialoguing, We can make this eulogy alive by reliving it through the dialogues.

We should start praising someone who deserves to be praised, or even the ones not deserving. Who knows you might change that person for the better. Actually, the laymen who practice this kind of honoring is called "roasting". Most celebrities practice this tradition especially for those who have great achievements in the movie industry for so long, for those working in the corporate world and for the retirees. They are given honors by roasting them. Positive comments must be encouraged and not negative ones.

There is this tradition or maybe cultural practice by a Charismatic group of honoring a member. They honor the birthday celebrants during their small prayer group meetings. The birthday celebrant will be sitting on a chair and everyone takes turn to say something positive and of course good comments to the celebrant. The comments can be something she/he has observed from the time they met this person. In other words, the first good impression, or anything they want to say positively or any reasons for giving the honor. It is a great feeling and heartfelt gratitude to hear beautiful things about yourself, isn't it?

There is a saying in our country that says "What is the use of the bundle of grass (feeds for the horse) if the horse is already gone and lifeless." So, when there is a chance to say something good to somebody say it now!

Another thing is, why do we feel so much guilt in our hearts when someone dies? One of the reasons is, because of the words left unsaid and deeds undone.

Now, isn't it true that when we say good things or simple "I love you" to someone at her/his dying bed, we feel at peace and very light inside our hearts? So, let us start saying things we want to say to somebody now, especially the good things about them.

Eulogy is to honor someone with sincerity. No matter how sincere the honoring is, the recipient won't be able to hear the honoring words anymore. The people who could only hear those honoring words are the ones who are at the funeral service.

I tell you what…why don't we start telling the people we love, that we love them. Would you like that? Not only one time but as frequent as possible. I have an inspirational poem for you entitled, "TELL IT NOW." This will guide you in preparing for any eulogy (yours or theirs) or to anybody you like or love. Allow me to start saying " GOD loves you and so do I."

Communication is essential for couples, parents, children, between friends and for everyone. It is important to express your love or fondness, to show them that you care. So tell them whatever it is...NOW.

TELL IT NOW

Three simple words, "I love you" tell it now
You hurt someone, "I'm sorry" tell it now
You want reconciliation, "Please forgive me" tell it now
You found out that your friend is ill, "I hope you feel better," tell it now
Your spouse cook something special for you, "thank you dear," tell it now
Your co-worker was just promoted, "Congratulations" tell it now
Your kid just got an "A+", "Good job kiddo,"tell it now
Your prayers are answered, "Thank You LORD," tell Him now

Words of encouragement

Words of compliment

Words of gratitude

Tell it now

But most of all. "LORD, thank You for everything"
Tell Him now, now is the time and do it all the time.

Let me ask you this, what would you feel if someone praise you or give you good comments or compliments on what you did? Of course there would be delight in your heart, right?

In Philippians 4: 8, it says "Finally, brothers, whatever is true, whatever is honorable, whatever is just, whatever is pure, whatever is lovely, whatever is gracious, if there is any excellence and if there is anything worthy of praise, think about these things. Yes, this Bible verse will guide us on how to honor somebody we love.

If you want to know how you stand in your circle of friends, in your family, or with your co-workers, or even in the community, start giving value to the little or short praises, the good comments or any pleasant words address to you.

I have a workable suggestion to help us in increasing our self-esteem, to feel better of ourselves and of course to know where we stand amongst the people around us. Remember, eulogy is for the living ears, not for the lifeless ears.

First, let me ask you, are you aware of what Pandora's Box is? It is an artifact in Greek Mythology taken from the myth of Pandora's creation. The box was actually a large jar. It may have been made of clay or bronze metal given to Pandora which contained all the evils of the world. This time we are going to change the contents of the Pandora's Box to something pleasant. Now we will have our own Pandora's box and it's not going to be a jar but a shoe box, (this is the kind I am using.) I know you've been receiving beautiful cards, all sorts of cards, notes on small papers or stationaries, and even memos with up-lifting messages written on them which sometimes you just throw away, right? The birthday cards with well wishes, anniversary cards with sweet sentiments, cards for Mother's Day or Father's Day, and from the upper person with promotional messages with his/her signatures must be kept. What are these things telling you? They are saying that you are a special person. If somebody tells you that you're special when you're already gone, it's not going to mean anything because you won't hear it anymore.

Again, please save those "testimonies of love" and keep them safe in the box. For me it should be one of the most treasured keepsakes. Don't you know that whatever is written on those cards and notes GOD is delighted because He created you in His Image? (Ponder on this.) He knows that there's goodness in everyone's heart.

I also would like to share that in my volume II of What's In My Heart?, my nephew (Francis) wrote me a very touching description of me through writing it in ABC manner. I have a chapter in that book that pertains to a lot of ABC such as ABC of Motherhood, ABC of How To Pray, etc., He wrote me the ABC of ESTHER and I included it in my book. Remember this is not about me. This is about honoring your loved ones. How about you? Why not get a shoe box and fill it with goodies of sef-worthiness. Don't discard the notes and beautiful cards with beautiful messages about you. This is a good model for anybody who wants to honor somebody.

When I feel blue and sad, or sometimes depressed, I open my Pandora's box and re-read the notes and cards. I feel better after that. You see when we're gone we can't take that box with us, but the memories will be left, this is the best eulogy for me. At least you know where you stand and you can be better. This is a nourishment for the soul.

There's another way to honor the deceased, (your loved ones), that is to perform a necrological service, like the one given for the Fallen 44. These were group of 44 police officers, (PNP- SAF) *Philippine National Police-Special Action Force,* who died last January 25,2015 in Mamasapano, Maguindanao, Philippines. It is a tragic event and we could feel there was not enough time to have a preparation for the unexpected death. There was a eulogy, but not done individually and so the honoring was done in collective way. In this case there were 4-5 people who gave their speeches. These were mostly political representative and higher officials. Some relatives were given the chance to say something in behalf of their deceased relatives.

I would like to offer my prayers for them and I will continue offering my silent prayer for all of them as long as I live. May all of them rest in peace and let Perpetual light shine upon them.

Eulogy mostly pertains to memories. The memories of the deceased are magnified and being spoken of. We missed our loved ones and we are adamant in our recollection of their memories. I have a beautiful and heartfelt poem for you to be treasured and to serve as a reminder about our loved ones.

THE TIME THAT WE MISSED

We have a lot of memories playing in our minds
The good and the bad, the glad and the sad
We tend to ignore the good part of it and
We feel the time that we missed.
In our hearts we regret the time that we missed
We take for granted the good acts that can be spared
We think everything is fine and nothing is wrong
Of just letting the time passes on
The moments of silence is important to us
To ponder and wonder on why such things happen?
Then you realize that in your solitude you know that
The time that you missed is the time you m i s s e d.
I do not want to linger on the hurt that was inflicted
In my heart I need to forgive and forget
Time will be there for the inner healing
The time that we missed in the midst of the grief.
Not only the grief that I needed to be healed
The emotional pain that was circling indeed
The nostalgic moments that I felt and missed
Was, my another year of birth
I will miss the memories of my beloved mother
I will treasure every moment of her love and care
I will pray as I have promised unceasingly for her
And I will wait for the time of her seeing our Creator
LORD GOD, Almighty, I lift up to you my mother
That You may soon welcome her in Your kingdom
The Eternal Heaven, where she would have a lasting
Peace in her heart and we know that the time we
Missed is the time she wished, "to be with You forever."

November 24, 2009 was my saddest birthday. I was looking at my mother's beautiful face and told her I would miss her so much and yes the time that I missed is the time that our family missed. When I wrote this poem my father was still alive. Then after 11 months later he passed away, too.

Actually this poem is for both of them. Whatever was in my heart, they all pertained to my father as well. We missed them.

CHAPTER IV

Life Is Too Short

Three years from now I will be almost two-thirds of a century old (70 years.) True, I am not getting any younger. This is the stage where the fear of dying surfaces. When my parents passed away, I started thinking about my own life of survival.

I started praying for their souls unceasingly in which I wish the same thing for my soul when my time comes. I even requested my nieces and nephews to continue praying (unceasingly too) for my soul when I depart from this earth. Sometimes, I am thinking of starting to pray for my own soul, but is that possible? I believe it's not possible to pray for someone's soul unless he/she is dead because we are to pray for that soul to be released from the purgatory. We can still pray for the person's souls but with different intentions this time. It is for the living ones. Anyway, for me, praying for the souls is very important, essential and rewarding. The reward is a place for us in heaven. Not only the praying for the souls are rewarded of heaven. Investing good deeds is another way to deserve the reward. Another important reminder is to be obedient in following the will of our Almighty.

In Matthew 7:21 it says, "Not everyone who says to me LORD, LORD, will enter the Kingdom of Heaven, but only the one who does the will of my Father in Heaven.

We know that GOD Has plans for us, for our own welfare. I believe we should reciprocate GOD with our plans too. The plans I am referring to is the plan of transformation. The bottom line is, whatever GOD's plan for mankind is, it is toward His Plan of Salvation. The time is NOW. I always say," Life is too Short, let's not make it shorter." The way I look at this world, it's not the age that counts when you want **a quality life.**

It is what you do with the time GOD is giving you. And it is also the sincerity of following the will of GOD.

My mother passed away in November 19, 2009 and my father passed away in October 26, 2010, so eleven months apart. From the time they were gone, my life has changed. I seldom get out of the house and I kept journaling whatever I was feeling and this helped me in my coping and in my grieving.

My constant journaling led me to publish my second book, "What's In My Heart vol. 1. I added the last chapter entitled," Lamentations" as the finishing touch of that book. And this was, when I was grieving. Indeed it was a great help in my everyday coping. So my book was published and followed by three more books, a total of four books within that time.

Coping is the key to moving on. I am blessed with expressing my inner feelings through writing poems. So my coping is a smooth sailing. Remember... Life Is Too Short to take it for granted and I am utilizing my gift from GOD.

Last year (2014) of February we had a golden jubilee high school reunion which was held in the Philippines. After two months of coming back here in the United States, I heard that one of my female classmates died. She was diagnosed with cancer of the cervix stage IV.

Another friend of ours that we haven't seen for almost five years was hospitalized last Summer and we didn't even know. He died of cancer of the prostate.

My sister-in-law's one year death anniversary was this July. Last year she passed away and also was diagnosed with cancer of the lungs.

A member of the Handmaids of the LORD, (a Catholic Charismatic group) passed away with cancer of the breasts.

The truth is, yes, it's a coincidence that they all died of cancer. It is true that there are more than a million ways to die. It is also true that closed to that number is, people with fear of dying. The bottom line is, no one in this world is exempted to live forever. We will all die and no doubt about that. The thing we can do is, we must pray all the time to have a peaceful death and to die in a state of grace. Again, Life Is Too Short.

Another thing is, we should start investing good deeds, on earth. The good news is"it's not too late" yet because heaven can wait. Again, life is too short, let's not make it shorter. Let's live our lives to the fullest.

As I have mentioned earlier, "coping" is the key to moving on. One of the ways to treasure our life is not to dwell on the past. We should look forward to a better world, a world where we can hear and listen to GOD's Word.

So, what are we going to do to move on? I have an inspiring poem for you entitled, "Let's Move On." Ponder on this please.

LET'S MOVE ON

Have you tried to step forward and
All of a sudden you step back?
Do you sweat on small stuff?
Do you have a rewinding mind and
Always dwell on the past?
Are you aware of the phrase,
"Let's move on"?
Yes, let's move on to a better future
Let's move on to a wider range,
The wider range of opportunities
And fortune,
Let's move on with our own life that
Brings forth indeed a fortitude
The hurt, the pain, we suffered in the past
Must be buried in the world of oblivion

We now can survive any upcoming storm
Because our past taught us a lesson
Let's move on with a brisk positive decision
The bitterness that stained our hearts
Must be washed out with our love
Let's forgive and try to forget
In order to move on and be reconciled
We grieved for our loss, we utmost-ly
Sighed and shed tears
We pondered on their memories
Shall we hold on to these?
Let's move on and face our fears
Behind our fears and uncertainties is,
Our LORD CHRIST JESUS
He is with us in our every move
He is there in our grief, even in our
Unpleasant moods
So, let's move on with the assurance
Of our LORD's compassion, The Greatest Companion.

Life is too short, yes, and I think we need to know more about our place in the future. We have to work on our way to heaven. We need to know more about the steps in reaching our heavenly goal.

Going back to the topic "Purgatory," I have a very important information about it. There are great favors that can be done for the dead person for his quick release from the punishment of Purgatory. Prayers can be said, the Holy Mass can be offered, and penances can be performed. These are solid offerings that are needed for more souls to be released from the Purgatory.

When St. Augustine was asked why he prayed so much for the dead, he replied *"I pray for the dead in order that when they reach heaven, they may pray for me."* I have this belief in my heart too, and I really believe there is faithfulness in it.

One of the most consoling Catholic teachings is the doctrine of the Communion of Saints, the grand and wondrous doctrine of our fellowship with souls in Purgatory.

In my life, I didn't have many enemies. Maybe I had at least 2-3 people, that I can remember. Actually, I don't need to address them as enemies, they are friends or acquaintances whom I had misunderstanding with and we just splitted without proper closure. I am a person who don't want to have misunderstanding with anybody and I guessed most people too. Had I known their whereabouts I would give effort to get in touch with them and ask for forgiveness. In the same token, I would forgive those people that have hurt me. Forgiveness is the key to attaining peace. Life is too short and forgiveness helps a person to have clear conscience. It promotes harmonious relationship between people, it strengthens and unites family ties.

One thing sure in my life nowadays is, I am learning to forgive and I am making sure I am also forgiven. We should learn to forgive and experience how it feels. Forgiveness has a melting effect in people's life.

I have two poems for you and me entitled "The Power Of Forgiveness," and "To Forgive Is...To Let Go."

THE POWER OF FORGIVENESS

We dwell on the past, we dwell on the hurt
We don't have peace, try to forgive
See the power of forgiveness.
We ignore the truth, we ignore the chance
We look for peace, try to forgive
See the power of forgiveness.
We take for granted the people around us
We failed to acknowledge our loved ones
We still seek for peace, try to forgive
See the power of forgiveness.
You have forgiven someone,

You have accepted the apology
But have you asked for forgiveness, too?
Try to ask for forgiveness,
And see how peaceful it is.
JESUS suffered for us and ransomed our sins
He taught us to forgive, not once
But more than seventy times
try to forgive and be forgiven,
Because the power of peace is
In the power of forgiveness.
Peace! Peace! Peace!

TO FORGIVE IS…TO LET GO

The hurt and pain and the heartaches I feel
The sorrows that still linger
The sleepless nights are still there
All these feelings are indeed real.
I tried to cope with unexpected news
I cried and shouted at the top of my voice
I was angry and full of hatred
For a while I was losing myself
I was craving for the inner healing
I poured out my sentiments to GOD
I asked the help of the Holy Spirit
And our Mother Mary to intercede
Thank You, LORD, thank you our
Blessed Mother
For the inner healing that I attained
For the gift of forgiveness and peace
And I am letting go of my ill-feelings
And letting GOD enter into my heart.

After reading the two poems, we'll be reminded again that indeed LIFE IS TOO SHORT.

There's something we need to consider in forgiving, that is, we should also need to forget and need to let go.

Actually, forgiving without forgetting is as good as not forgiving at all. It is not possible you may say, but with GOD's grace and (you must ask for it), everything will be in its proper place. He will help you to forgive and to forget as well. So learn to forgive and to forget and you'll earn your peace.

Are you aware why you can forgive and can't just forget? I have my own theory of why? The heart is the one responsible for forgiving because we can teach our hearts to forgive. Our mind dictates our hearts but our mind does the recollection and subconsciously it controls on what to think. The unpleasant incidents just pop up in our minds and make us recall the unforgivable events. Well, the most important thing is that, our hearts overpower the goodness side and backed-up with humility.

Let me share with you what's behind the gift of humility. First, you'll find joy. Second you'll have contentment and third, you'll have peace in your heart. These three virtues can be experienced only when you learn to forgive and when you learn to acknowledge your own mistakes as well as when you learn to ask for forgiveness. Humility is the acknowledgement of the truth and the absolute foundation of spiritual life. So cultivate more virtues now and practice them toward others because (Life Is Too Short.)

Have a good life with GOD's love!

CHAPTER V

Lamentations

Lamentation is a healthy emotional outlet for releasing our emotional tensions through wailing, moaning, groaning and weeping. Lamenting helps us in grieving. For deeper spiritual aspect, lamentation is a collective heartfelt sounds of sighs.

In the Book of Lamentations, it portrays the Israel's crisis, the destruction of the temple, the interruption of it's ritual, and the exile of the leaders and lost of national sovereignty.

When my parents passed away, I had a very good amount of lamentation that brought relief in my entire grieving, and it is a healthy one. In my lamentation, I had the chance to write what's in my heart. I have expressed my emotions and feelings (a total grief) in a healthy way.

For me, writing poems/poetry is a form of lamentation. Indeed, while I was writing I was weeping, sobbing and even talking aloud to myself, to my parents' portraits, to my kinship and to the sky sometimes. Mind you, those were good ventilation of emotion and burden releasers. Thank You my LORD for Your love and care. Thank You for allowing me to lament. My constant writing of what I feel during my grief helped me a lot in my healing and grieving process. I poured out my heartaches and pains in writing messages, poems and poetry and a lot of journaling.

I know in some aspects of your life, you have experienced loss, if not a relative, a pet maybe or something very important to you. Hurt is hurt, so allow me to share my lamentations with you. It's ok to share and talk to friends or confidants about how you feel and how you are coping.

A shared grief indeed lessens the burden. The beautiful thing about GOD's love and mercy for us is He cares about our sorrowful heart.

When you lose someone near the holiday season, like Christmas (such as in my case) the more difficult it is to grieve because there are more memories to ponder on. In order for me to go on while grieving I kept thinking of JESUS because He is the reason for the season. Let me share with you this lovely poem for a Holiday grief.

CHRISTMAS BEYOND THE GRIEF

T'was the day when the loved ones passed away
T'was the time to process the normal grief
T'was the moment to ponder their memories
Yes, grief is a feeling that cannot be expressed.
Christmas is the time to celebrate by all
It is the season long awaited for
It is the birth of the new born king
The Infant in a manger, soon to be the Redeemer.
Have you ever felt the pain of sadness?
During the season of advent?
Did you know of someone who might be feeling blue?
Does Christmas give the chills of emptiness?
Yes, there is such Christmas beyond the grief.
Let me share with you how I feel this season
It pains me to have lost my parents within a year
It intensifies the longing-ness of their presence
But it granted me the strength and gift of acceptance
The Bible says, *"there is a season for everything"*
A time to be born, a time to die, a time to cry
A time to laugh, a time to mourn and a time to dance.
And I say, "there's a time to heal and a time to put
The broken pieces together.
Through this Christmas season the inner healings begin
Because beyond my grief there is the gift of JESUS
The only reason for the season.

Moving on is a healthy way to cope from any grief, broken relationship, or any sort of failures. Sometimes we don't know how to cope and sometimes we don't know what directions we are going to follow.

I am supposed to include in this chapter the poem entitled, "The Time That We Missed," but I chose to have it at "Eulogy" chapter.

Since I am personalizing most part of my book, I would like to share my personal experience. This is about one of my dreams. I believed that dreams can help released some hidden aggressions or tensions. Dreams can fulfill some wishes. Remember the saying "Dreams come true;" (wishes come true in dreams.) Now, I can testify that Dreams Heal as told in the following story.

DREAMS HEAL

One of the things that helps me in my grieving process is my dream and the sequence of my dreams.

Few weeks after my mother passed away, I dreamed of her, and it was a pleasant one, that she cooked my favorite food. And in one of my dreams, I was still crying hard, and trying to let her know how much I loved her and missed her. It seemed so real that I felt like I was talking to her. Another dream was she smiled at me while I was painting. My father passed away and joined my mother after eleven months. Mind you, both of them were in my dreams now.

One vivid dream was, I indeed felt the warmth of my mother. She hugged me so tight and she even uttered,"Don't worry daughter, your father and I are in good hands.' While she was saying that, I glanced at my father who was sitting on his rocking chair and saw him smiling, agreeing with what my mother was saying. I am happy to have dreamt about them. It was a great consolation seeing them, talking to them and feeling their warmth in my dreams. I look forward for more scenes of my encounter with them and for more dialogues with them in my dreams. I strongly believe that dreams heal, aid in the process of inner healing and grieving process.

Thank You LORD for the gift of dream.

Honestly, I have been dreaming about my mother and father until now. Everytime I dream of them, there's a delight and joy in my heart. It is making my day. Sometimes, it felt real, like that time when I really felt the warmth of my mother's hugs and embraces. At one point I was having a conversation with my father and I was really listening to his advice. He was very attentive when I was telling him my concerns. Again, try to ask GOD for the gift of dreams.

Lamentations are not just for human beings. Even animals, they also lament. Elephant is a typical example. The elephant herd are matriachs.

The mother elephants are the heads of the herds. When one dies, the elephants cover the dead body with leaves, twigs and branches. Then at night time, they walk circling around the breathless elephant moaning, groaning, weeping, wailing and with tears in their eyes. I have a message for you from a mother elephant -

> It pains me to lose someone I loved
> I am heavy and huge but with soft heart
> Time like this I need to keep silent
> Yes, I need a space to lament.

I thought lamentation is just part of grieving and just a temporary thing. But in *the Book of Lamentations 3:40-41, it says 40 Let us search and examine our ways that we may return to the LORD; 41 Let us reach out our hearts toward GOD in heaven!*

The Bible verses are very clear, that we need to examine our ways. I will say it again, we have to invest good deeds here on earth. Isn't it that when we keep quiet, when we are silent and even when we lament, there are moments that are given to us just to ponder? Yes, moments to ponder on what we are doing in this world? What do we need to do to live our life to the fullest? Whatever we do on this earth is measured and accounted for. (that is on how we treat other people.) Whatever we do, reflects the way we live. Now, let me remind you again to invest kindness and goodness here on earth so you can attain the rewards in Heaven. Investing good deeds is a very noble act..

When we are in a sad mood and when we feel the burden of pain, that's the beginning of mind struggle. When we lament the things in our minds and when feel the pain in our hearts, we tend to question every little thing?

There is an absolute answer to this struggle as mentioned. In *the Book of Lamentations 3:21-25, it says 21 "But I will call this to mind, as my reason to have hope, 22 The favors of the LORD are not exhausted, his mercies are not spent; 23 They are renewed each morning, so great is his faithfulness, 24 My portion is the LORD, says my soul; therefore will I hope in him. 25 Good is the LORD to one who waits for him, to the soul that seeks him."*

Knowing that there is a constant help from GOD and His promise of hope, the more it is important to lament in silence, as it says *in the Book of Lamentations 3:26, "It is good to hope in silence for the saving help of the LORD.* In silence, you will feel more the Presence of GOD, and when you feel His Presence, that is the best time to lament. We realize that when lamenting, the only thing we will hear is the moaning, wailing, groaning and weeping. GOD knows all the meaning of these lamentation sounds. I believe that lamentation is one of the gifts of the Holy Spirit since He also gave us the gift of tongues.

To close this chapter, allow me to emphasize that in Lamentations, you'll be given the chance to have close communion with our LORD. And then, you'll be given the time to ask for forgiveness. So let the pride in your heart be replaced with humility. Remember that when you lament, this is a sign of surrendering, and surrendering is offering your humbleness.

CHAPTER VI

Inspirational Insights

In this world we need inspirations to drive us to do better; to reach our goals with satisfaction, to do the right thing and to be what we are with ourselves. This chapter will give us insights to inspire us like the Holy Spirit who inspires me. Let's inspire each other through the Holy Spirit's generosity. Are we in, with the Inspirational Insights?

It's time for us to reflect, time for us to have realization of how insightful our lives can be. It's time for us to have awareness of the natural and supernatural occurrences in this mysterious world, including the miracle of life and the mystery of death.

My life will be dull and it would be like a "black and white" movie film, without the inspirational insights. It would be like the world of zombies. The truth is, one of my favorite movies is about zombies. That's why I am avid fan of the television series,"The Walking Dead". It is a very colorful film with red bloody scene all the time. Unlike the first zombie film it was in black and white film. Allow me to be humorous once in a while. My concept of inspirational insight is just like a colored movie that adds color to ones life. I am hungry for inspirational insights. They make me stronger in my faith, allowing me to be open to receive the Holy Spirit's gifts and be aware of my surroundings. The most important thing is knowing the essence of receiving the gifts of the Holy Spirit. One essential aspect is attaining my peace and contentment.

Do you believe in GOD's will and prompts of the Holy Spirit? I do. If you go with the prayer of (asking GOD's will and thanking the Holy Spirit's prompts), the result would be "holy discernment". This is what I do, relying everything on the prompts of the Holy Spirit and following

GOD's will in my life. You may ask how do I know if it's GOD will and prompts of the Holy Spirit.

Yes, we would know. Just believe in the Holy Spirit, have a strong faith and let you heart speaks. Pray is the key to all of this. Pray!Pray!Pray!

Lately, I have been mentioning in this book about my inner thoughts mostly about death. I never thought of writing another book again. I had a lot of thoughts and feelings regarding death and fear. I prayed about it, prayed for it and all of a sudden, I looked for a blank paper at home and I was prompted to write these phrases, "Deep Inner Thoughts, Concept Of Death, Overcoming Fear." Then I thought of using this as the title of another book and this will be my seventh book.

Now, let me ask you this, how can we attain inspirational insights?

Being resourceful is one good answer. I believe that this is one of my strong qualities. I am not satisfied without probing, investigating and even researching to find the truth, to look for remedies and of course to resolve any issues. Inspirational insights are the keys for better living. Part of the inspirational insights are relying on GOD's will and His power.

Another way to attain inspirational insights is learning to cultivate virtues. We cannot just grab virtues. We have to earn them and be open and most of all develop interest in cultivating them. Virtues are like silver, gold and diamond. They are very precious that needed to be treasured. If not for the inspirational insights, I won't be able to survive my depression, the trials in my life, and all the struggles that I went through.

One time, my brother told me that every time he hears the songs, "The "Impossible Dream", and "Climb Every Mountain" he is reminded him of me, that I would always try to reach the unreachable star and meet my goals. I would tackle every crampled paper and straighten it out which means I am a trouble shooter, an analogy for being me.

Another brother of mine shared to the family that if ever I would be lost in the jungle, I would survive because I am a quick thinker and resourceful. Well, enough for being a survivor and a trouble shooter. I appreciate the things they were saying about me but I believe in my heart that everything that is happening in my life is GOD's will. He is the only One who is helping, guiding and providing 100% of everything in my life – (the means to survive and that includes the inspirational insights.) Through the inspirational insights, I am able to discern on what to do with what I want to do. I am able to feel peace and contentment. I can be bold in saying that in His Presence I can face the uncertainties, more so with death. Another way to attain inspirational insights is to keep reading inspirational books. One thing sure is that, the main reason why I was able to come out with 5-6 books is, my continuous reading variety of books. My interest in reading paid off. Constant reading results in harvesting wisdom. I am grateful that reading is my favorite hobby. Last, but not the least, the utmost source of these inspirational insights is GOD's wonderful gift… the gift of knowledge and the gift of wisdom. I am grateful for these wonderful gifts.

I know the consequences of the after effect of chemotherapy and radiation and I believed that the inspirational insights that I attained is "I am always guided by the Holy Spirit; and that our Blessed Mother is strongly interceding for me and with me; JESUS is my strong backer and GOD is my Redeemer. Cancer or no cancer? with or without chemotherapy or radiation, THEY ARE WITH ME. I have the full support from the Holy People.

Relatives, friends and communities are also my inspirations in life. I am thankful for the boldness and braveness that I received from GOD, especially the replacing of my Fear to Faith…my boldness of sharing my concept of death. Now, let me shower you with more inspirational insights. These are just brown bags that you can carry with you. These are few poems that you can glance at and maybe you can share to a person standing infront of you.

With all the struggles that I have faced in my life, I really owed my victory of survival from our Almighty. I would say that GOD is enough in all life's battle especially my own. Just to think that GOD is enough, it is already a very strong coping mechanism. It is the only solution and enough solution. This is the Best answer to all our struggles and trials…

GOD IS ENOUGH

We are in this world to live and die
We ought to know the how and why
We have our conscience to follow through
But do we really know what to do?
We question ourselves and wonder at times
On how we can survive the daily tasks
But we always forget that no matter what
GOD IS ENOUGH, we should remember that.
Yes, GOD is enough and the enough answer
To all the doubts and personal concerns
All we have to do is to acknowledge His Presence
Then the contentment and peace will be there.
Yes, GOD IS ENOUGH and His love stands out
His love is enough to hold on tight
GOD IS ENOUGH and we should know that
So let's start putting our GOD in our hearts
(To be the first and not our last.)
Again, GOD IS ENOUGH…

One line of the title of my book is "Overcoming Fear"… Overcoming anything is indeed a challenge, so we really need an insight to reinforce the overcoming defense mechanism. Facing realities, facing challenges and facing struggles are the battles that we are forced to tackle. So, let's see what does it says about Overcomer?

OVERCOMER

It's indeed true, that GOD won't give us things we
can't handle, for He teaches us to be an overcomer.
GOD is always there, in trials and tribulations
He guides us every step of the way
He shows the way to be an overcomer.
So stop complaining, stop blaming
Start trusting, start believing
These are the steps to overcoming.
Be an overcomer and ask GOD for the graces
Have a strong faith and believe that you can
handle the trials, for you are an overcomer.
Be proud of yourself, of your accomplishments
All these graces are from GOD Himself
So from now on, be an overcomer yourself.
Overcomer you become, faith you hold on
GOD is your strength and don't forget
Our LORD is the Best Overcomer.

Most of the time, we just take for granted the freedom that we have in this world.

When Adam and Eve were thrown out from the Garden of Eden, they left the place with the privilege of choosing between good and evil. And that was the start of chaos in Paradise. They allowed temptation to interfere and they faced its consequences. They begun to walk on a thorny road. They live with their mark… the mark of sin. From a bright surrounding, of the Paradise, there was a big change in the life of the original couple. Darkness started to surround them.

I have a poem supposedly for Adam and Eve, but this would be for all of us, (the symbolism of the first couple.) This poem is entitled "IN DARKNESS." This is for everyone, a couple or not, to inspire them in handling their lives in a day to day basis.

IN DARKNESS

We live in the world of beauty
We appreciate the nature around us
We see from our eyes different movements
We are lucky, we are able to see things
Let us honor the blind for their hearts
For their hope and perseverance, too
They only see things from their hearts,
Darkness, they don't even know how it looks
Gloomy weather, heavy burden and feelings
Signs of hopelessness and helplessness
Feelings of shrinking and passing through
the tunnel, unpleasant, negative, destructive,.
that's darkness.
In the beginning of creation, light and darkness
were created, and they were also separated
for certain reason
All these were GOD's accomplishments
in six days, then He created the day and
night and He was pleased.
The first couple did have a bright life
Until they were tempted and committed a sin
That was then, the start of darkness
And sin was the manifestation of living
in the dim.
We see the sun at daytime, so radiant
We see the stars and the moon at night,
So brilliant
We can appreciate the brilliance in darkness
And that's how you should take darkness
in your life, In your aloneness, loneliness,
lowliness, in the darkness of your life, just
watch for the rays of the light in which
within your reach

It is GOD Who brightens your day and
your way, no more darkness,
no more dimness, let the peace and
calmness surround you
Always think that GOD is always there
to shine us through the darkness,
Longing for the light
We are reassured of the light of CHRIST JESUS
The light of JESUS will come into the world
To guide us and lead us to the Kingdom of GOD

Look around us, we see the beauty of nature, and we see the reality of poverty. We see and hear the news about the calamities and disasters in the remote areas and even in the near-by cities. The news are full of crimes and accidents such as car accidents, gun shots, and other mishaps. How about the fire, the flood, the typhoons, the earthquakes and not to forget the tsunamis. Inspite of these, there are people who are cheerful and in their hearts they are grateful, because they focus on the good things. Allow me to share with you these inspirational poems to counteract the unpleasant and the negative vibes that engulf around us.

Are you ready now to read the "Focus On The Good Things" and

"Something To Look Forward To…?"

FOCUS ON THE GOOD THINGS

We are in this world with a lot of challenges
We have to face the reality whatever it takes
We are at the verge of losing our grip
Why don't we focus on the good things?
Calamities of different sort are always in the news
We have the eathquakes, the hurricanes and the
tornadoes
Not to forget the accidents, the crimes and other
mishaps
We really need to focus on the good things.
The war is still going on, a national concern
There are family rivalries, feuds and broken homes
Terminal illnesses and the chronic diseases
Trigger our normal life and its essence
The more we need to focus on the good things.
We feel frustrated, depressed and stressed
of our daily routine tasks and activities
We are engrossed and overwhelmed with
our success
Still we don't have contentment and peace
Again, try to focus on the good things
The good things are not about the materials
and fame it is about the hope, the belief and
the faith we have
It is about the coming of our CHRIST JESUS,
Our Savior
And His promise of our Eternal Salvation
So be not afraid of all the terrible things
going on
Just focus on the good things and put

this powerful verse *(Luke 21:11)* in
your heart, for you to ponder on
at any given moment.

In Luke 21:11 it says,"There will be powerful earthquakes, famines and plagues from place to place, and awesome sights and mighty signs will come from the sky."

If we focus on the good things, our tendency is to have something to look forward to,right? If we have something to look forward to, there is a great hope of handling things in a positive way. This poem entails the riches and abundance of our Almighty, and all we need to do is, to claim them and work on them.

SOMETHING TO LOOK FORWARD TO

The morning comes and joins the sun to say,
"Good-day"
A prayer offered up high and this I say
Thank You my LORD for today's plan
And hold my hands as we walk on this land.
LORD, I do not know where to go
But I do know that I will follow You
Today is another day of appreciation
A thanksgiving gesture, my contribution
When I wake up in the morning
I feel the joy in my heart,
In my heart I can feel Your
Presence a real delight
So my LORD, here is my sincere desire
To be with You, and be my guide.
I have my strength that I can use
Because You are the Source of my virtues
I know that as I open my eyes

There's something to look forward to…
I can't deny
I feel the peace, I have faith, I strongly
Believe that hope takes care of all these
There's always something to look forward to…
Like the great plan of salvation
Shall we hold on our Hope, the One
And only Savior of mankind.

Whatever you do in your life, always think that Somebody is watching you and guiding you as well. Just trust Him and have faith in His Presence. Who else but our Almighty GOD that is behind our daily endeavors. In this chaotic world, we really need spiritual guidance to survive the turmoils, the trials, the tribulations and the struggles in life. We should always ask for a spiritual tenacity and if we have attained this, it will take care of the physical, emotional, psychological and even the moral aspect of our life. Just don't doubt the power of GOD. Never, never doubt.

NEVER DOUBT

The Holy Spirit is within you, never doubt
The love and mercy within reach, never doubt
GOD Has a plan for everyone, never doubt.
Never doubt a single drop
Never doubt in your life
That JESUS will come any moment.
The doubt that you have, leave it in oblivion
The sign of miracles have been witnessed
The seeing of the blind, the walking of the
Lame, the cure of the illness
All of these and many more will sweep
The dust of your doubts
Even the power of casting evil, you can
Perform, just say, "In the Name of JESUS"
I cast you demon

Never doubt, that it will go away and
Will be gone
Never doubt, the power of GOD is in
Your heart
Change your doubt to devotion and ask
GOD for this grace
You will be given faith and belief and
obedience at the end
Yield to the Holy Spirit and see it for
yourself
So never doubt, never doubt the power
Of GOD and the power of love.

Do you have struggles currently? Did you ask for the help of the Almighty?
Do you have a "struggling heart?" I would like share the following poem
with you-

MY STRUGGLING HEART

My heart speaks of our gripes and pains
My heart craves for the consoling words
My heart strives for an utmost peace
Yes, I do have a struggling heart
I ask GOD to see my heart
I beg Him to feel my pain
I seek for His mercy and love
I want Him to touch my struggling heart
LORD, this I beg for You to give
Fill my heart with Your wisdom
Fill my heart with humility
Fill my heart with Your love and mercy
Fill my heart with serenity
Fill my heart with understanding
Fill my heart with forgiveness
Fill my heart with inner healing

Fill my heart with peace
Yes my LORD fill me, my whole being
With holiness and worthiness
Fill my heart with tranquility, which
My heart longs to receive and this
Heart is yours to keep.

*I have mentioned earlier that another way to attain inspirational insights
is to cultivate virtues. Again, you can't just grab virtues. You have to earn
them. Virtues are the ingredients for inspirational insights. Virtues and
wisdom are cousins. Wisdom backs up the virtues that you are going to
utilize. So let's have a preview of what virtues are.*

VIRTUES

Good qualities, positive attitude, if you possess these,
You're a success
You've been patient, you're honest, that's the way
To run business.
Caring for people, rendering good service,
Catering to the right prospects
Virtues of any kind, very useful every time.
Random Act Of Kindness, grab it any chance moment
You will feel good and you'll be respected
Humility is another virtue and it's the best
Peace is the reward of all the efforts
You have endured.
Let us practice all the virtues we have received
And let us apply them in our daily encounters
Our lives will be better for we are on
the right track
Rest assured that our LORD GOD is always at our back.
VIRTUES PLUS EFFORT EQUALS INSPIRATIONAL
INSIGHTS AND BLESSED BY GOD'S WILL.

Everything that moves is alive, correct? No, not everything. Plants and flowers in the garden, sometimes don't move, but they are alive. That is an allegorical way to say, we need to slow down for a while, we need to be silent, and sometimes we need the time to retreat from the chaotic surroundings.

There are events in our lives that bring us joy and events that destroy certain relationships. There are times when our spirituality is getting away. I believe that we need sometime to retreat, to get away and be alone with GOD to keep our spirituality burning.

I wrote the following poem when I attended a retreat, two weeks after my mother passed away. I needed that time, a time to be alone with GOD. So here's a "Retreat Of Silence" for you.

RETREAT OF SILENCE

I came to be with You my LORD in the
Sanctuary of Your heart
I came to talk to You in the silence
I came to listen to Your voice so soft
Here I am LORD in the Retreat of Silence.
LORD, in here I started to reflect
I reflect on my old and existing sins
I searched for my lost soul indeed
And I seek for Your utmost forgiveness
Now that I am away from the city
Away from the noise and the turmoil
I now have time to be alone with You
To pour out myself, my pain and sorrow
In my heart there is heaviness
In my mind there is confusion
In this place I found myself and found
You, my LORD
Yes, my LORD, I am grateful to say
That I made the right discernment to be with

You in this Retreat of Silence
I know that in Your time, time heals.
And I feel You all the time, feel Your Presence
Thank You Father for embracing me
Thank You my Mother, the Blessed One
For interceding, thank you for allowing
me to be reconciled with You again
But most of all, thank You for I am again forgiven,
In Your name, I say and pray, Amen!

There are three things survivors look into and these are: Hope! Hope! Hope! If every single person leans on hope it would be a better world. There would be a higher rate of success in every dealings. The positive attitude will be enhanced. Hope is a sturdy foundation. So, would you choose a named "Hope" for your kid (daughter maybe) or to a huggable poodle or cuddly cat. Ain't that a beautiful name with such a graceful meaning? I have a soulmate named" Hope, the Deliverer of Hope, the Sovereign One. Now tell me, is there hope?

THERE IS HOPE

Quietly I ponder and question the validity of looking
positively at the meaning of life.
Doubts in my mind, thoughts occur
Hold on tight to the faith that was implanted
In my heart
That was the start of working on my hopes
Delight in my heart, feeling great as I smile
Looking at the sky, sending my message to the
Deliverer of Hope in this world
to reciprocate and confirm to Him,
that the Almighty, is the only genuine hope,
I learned to instill in my mind and drill in my heart
there is truly with no tinge of doubt
That There Is Hope.

You've gone through knowing what my book is all about and trying to understand each chapter's message. You have gathered some inspirational insights and inspirational poems, so now you would need moments for yourselves to ponder and feel the Presence of GOD. This, you can do in silence. Any moment in time is this…this is the moment.

THIS IS THE MOMENT

A moment like this is worth waiting for
A moment alone with You my LORD
Yes, this is the moment, a moment
To pour out what my thoughts are.
A moment to express what my heart
Desires, yes this is the moment
A moment of excitement, hearing
The Good News, a moment to reflect.
A moment of reconciliation with
someone or self, yes this is the moment
A moment for forgiveness, to forgive and
be forgiven, a moment long awaited for
A moment to tell the world, you're loved
By the Almighty and Sovereign One
Yes, this is the moment, to be aware of
Claiming the peace in our hearts forever!

I can't help but share more of my poems. The key word here is "inspirational". I am inspired all the time to write inspirational poems. I would like that whoever will read this book will be inspired too. I will forever thank the Holy Spirit for giving me such gifts. Let us continue to be open to the messages of our LORD through the Inspirational Insights that He implanted in our hearts. I have a very short message for us to ponder in the midst of <u>no where</u> where GOD <u>is now here</u>.

Esther B. Jimenez

IN THE MIDST

In the midst of this chaotic world
There is a room for peace
In the midst of the family feud
There is a harmonious relationship
In the midst of work rivalry, there is unity
And in the midst of brokenness
There are pieces to put together
In the midst of all, there is GOD
To depend on
Yes our LORD is in our midst
Now and forever.

CHAPTER VII

Understanding The Scriptures

Let us start with this Scripture from the Bible according to *2Peter 3:15-16 that says, 15 And consider the patience of our LORD as salvation, as our beloved brother Paul, according to the wisdom given to him, also wrote to you 16 speaking of these things as he does in all his letters. In them there are some things hard to understand that the ignorant and unstable distort to their own destruction, just as they do the other Scriptures.*

THE BIBLE IS YOUR LIFE, YOUR LIFE IS BIBLICAL

The Bible says a lot about death and resurrection. There are some Bible verses that inspired me. Some are strongly related to my experiences and situations. The verses that give me hope and a peaceful future are from *John 14:1-4 Do not let your heart be troubled. You have faith in GOD; have faith also in me, 2 In my Father's house there are many dwelling places. If there were not, would I have told you that I am going to prepare a place for you? 3 And if I go and prepare a place for you, I will come back again and take you to myself, so that where I am you also maybe 4 where I am going you know the way.* WHAT A REASSURANCE? These are inspiring verses, a promising one and a hopeful place to dwell in and a secured one to be in our Father's house, our final destination. I really feel the essence of the Scripture. For me it's not only everlasting stability… but a life after death.

I owe my spiritual tenacity from my stronghold of the Scriptures, from the powerful Word of the Almighty and the seed of faith that was planted in my heart. Let's look into the deep meaning of faith. In Hebrews 11:1-3 it says, 1Faith is the realization of what is hoped for and evidence of things not seen 2 Because of it the ancients were well attested 3 By faith we understand that the universe was ordered by the Word of GOD, so that what is visible came into being through the invincible. Faith is one of the powerful virtues that led me to sturdy conviction. This helps me in the completion of of my "Deep Inner Thoughts, Concept Of Death, Overcoming Fear" book.

The following poem is an excerpt from the BIBLE TIDBITS and the title is "AMAZING BOOK".

THE AMAZING BOOK

Let us reflect on this verse about the Bible
The Bible is the best seller in the whole world
It tells the story of mankind and creation
And the origin of our parents and its generation
The Bible is a book of reference, a book of
Virtue, a book of knowledge.
It's a guide for everything and anything
You can imagine,
The proverbs, the psalms, the canticles of the
Prophets are just overwhelming and
Worth reading
So it's not too late yet fellow readers
Start opening your Bible, read it diligently
Ponder from your heart and reflective mind
And don't let your Bible stay on the shelf,
Stagnant just to accumulate dust.
Now, if you're weary, tired, worried and
Troubled, just open your Bible and ponder
On the Scriptures
There are wonderful passages that the Bible
Offers, and your troubles will turn into triumphs.

Reading the Word of GOD is fulfilling. You can't go wrong. It changes a lot of people. We have known from a lot of testimonies, from a lot of inmates about how they spend their time in prison. Most of them claim that they started reading the Bible.

I am happy to include "Understanding the Scriptures" as one of the chapters because the Bible is our life and our life is Biblical. Without the Bible, I won't be able to know and understand how it is to live my life. Reading the Word of GOD in Scripture is different from ordinary reading of any articles. When I started reading the Bible, I learned to overcome a lot of my fears, I learned to cope with everyday challenges in my life, I understand the role of struggles that I am facing and most of all I have known that JESUS is our Savior.

One of the things that aids me in my present situation is listening to the heart of GOD. There is a Scripture-based prayer called, "Lectio-Divina."There are many more books that tell about Lectio-Divina in detail.

There are four steps included in Lectio- Divina that are Bible-based and this is an important and timeless way of feeling the Presence of our LORD.

First Step is, Read The Word...You might want to read the Sunday gospel or any verses that catch your attention in any religious book, or even in the Bible itself. Before you begin to read, ask the Holy Spirit's guidance, and pray the Holy Spirit prayer. Then begin with a moment of silence by turning your attention away from your daily concerns and be still and focus on GOD's Presence within you. The ancient monks called this step. "lectio" or reading.

Second Step is, Ponder the Word... To ponder is to reflect on it, to think about the meaning of the passage that you read in your life.Follow the Holy Spirit's prompts and allow GOD to feed you with the Word. This step is called, "meditatio" or meditation.

<u>Third Step</u> is, Respond To The Word… this is basically the prayer of the heart. We respond to GOD's Word spontaneously and silently from our hearts. This step is called, "oratio" or "prayer".

We consciously present our response to the LORD and let's allow our response to emerge. As Saint Augustine once said, " *You have made us for yourself, O LORD, and our hearts are restless until they rest in You."*

Pray as you can, not as you can't a basic principle to remember.

<u>Fourth Step</u> is, Surrender To The Word…this fourth step of prayer calls us simply to say, "Yes" to GOD. Like Mary who surrendered to the Word of GOD as proclaimed by the angel Gabriel. The traditional name of this step is "contemplatio" or contemplation. It is a gift from GOD, not something that we can produce in ourselves.

The goal of praying with Scripture is, to absorb the Word of GOD so completely into our lives that shapes our way of life and forms who we are. If we pray from our hearts, it will clear our mind and we can feel more the Presence of GOD.

With this "lectio divina" I am now experiencing calmness and clarity of my discernment. My uncertainties become certain, especially when I use my time in a constructive way. And this is a quality praying. I should not waste my precious time but try my best to use my valuable time with what GOD intends me to do with my life. When my time comes I would be as healthy as possible and ready to face our Creator with dignity and joy.

There is a verse in the Bible *in Romans 8: 16-17 that says, 16 GOD's Spirit joins himself to our spirits to declare that we are GOD's children. 17 Since we are his children we will possess the blessings he keeps for his people, and we will possess with CHRIST what GOD has kept for Him; for if we share CHRIST's suffering, we will also share his glory.* Understanding the Scriptures is to know GOD more and to know Him better. When you start to know GOD more, you would understand that GOD has a divine purpose for every challenge that comes our way. These challenges are intended to test our faith. Faith is very essential in handling fears. If not for my faith, I would be struggling until now with my unknown and known fears. I strongly believe that GOD is with me. I could feel His Presence. It's an awesome feeling just to know that whatever I do, GOD is there to help me through. Hope is keeping me alive with the strong faith, that I am in our LORD's hands.

I wasn't a prayerful person before. When my life started to transform, I started to lean on GOD for everything. And I was so thankful that I was called by our Almighty. When GOD calls us, He would guide us every step of the way. I was guided by the Holy Spirit. I started reading the Bible, and I pondered on it and I solely meditate on it. For me, the Bible is the best book, the all-knowing book, and the true book. If you have any questions about the facts of life, relationships, history of mankind and about everything, the Bible will give you the answers.

Understanding the Scriptures is the answer to understanding what's going on with your thoughts and feelings. The Scripture is centered directly to ones mind and ones heart. The Bible is a diversity, translated into different languages that unites the hearts and minds of mankind. Understanding the Scriptures is a universal teaching of who you are and knowing we are created in GOD's Image. Before I started to be engrossed with the Bible, I didn't know the meaning of parables in the New Testament. Now, I do understand each parable. Part of what I have learned in Understanding The Scriptures is writing some parables of my own, in which the messages are cultivating virtues and provoking our hearts and minds to respond. Here are some parables that I would like to share.

THE PARABLE OF WISDOM

In the land of the "Dreamer"
There is a dreamer roaming
He is fascinated with the
Riches around him
He is given the chance to pick
What he wants
But there is a condition
That he must comply
He is to use it every time
And share to everyone
For if he fails to do it
He is nothing but a real "Dreamer".

Virtues: Share Your Time, Talent and Treasure.

THE PARABLE OF PRAYER

Two little kids are in the playground
Talking to each other
One is a little boy and the other
Is a little girl
The girl asked the boy if he could
Sing a song
The boy gladly replied," Yes I can",
Do you want to hear?
The girl nodded.
"Jack and Jill went up the hill
To ask our GOD the Father,
Jack knelt down and bowed his head
To thank the LORD for his sweater
After that, Jill clasped her hands
And closed her eyes and asked GOD
To look after her kitten

So both kids smiled cheerfully
They part ways, leaving the beauty and
Wonders of prayers in their hearts,
Forever.Amen!

Virtues: No prayers from anyone and anybody left unanswered.

THE PARABLE OF OBEDIENCE

There is a widow with twin daughters
Both in their high school teens
One is good in Literature and Art
The other is good in Science and Math
These twins are vey studious
They always excel in every class
They have perfect attendance
They are always prepared in any exam
One weekend their mother asked one of them
To do the laundry, and to the other
To clean the pantry
They are engrossed with what they're doing
And ignored what their mother is saying
What good it is to be intelligent and with
Excellent grades, if you can't even show
Some kind of obedience?

Virtues: The key to a better Christian is to be obedient. Come to think of it…because of our Blessed Mother's obedience, we have JESUS in our lives.

THE PARABLE OF HOPE

An old turtle who lives in a cave
Came out one day
He walks, he looks around, he listens
And smells his surroundings

He talks to himself and with a smile
He says,"O how beautiful this earth is"!
He enjoys the snow in the Winter
He likes the scent of the flowers
In the Spring
He basks the whole Summer
And in the Fall, he plays with the leaves
He is there in a cave to contemplate
The beauty of everything that
GOD Has created.
What makes him live that long?
How heavy is the shell he carries along?
Why is he known as a slow creature?
The secret answer to those questions
Is his "hope" to live for the beauty of life"
And the "hope to carry on"

*Virtues: In Patience there is HOPE, in HOPE there is a reward
Patience is a VIRTUE.*

THE PARABLE OF GRIEF

A herd of elephants were running in the jungle
They were being chased by the poachers
The ground was shaken with the pounding
Steps of the herds
The parent elephants were trying to protect
The young ones by placing in between them.
Unfortunately there were at least three
Young ones that were killed
Since they were at their youthful age
The tusks are not useful, because they
Are not sellable, so the poachers left.
The herds grouped together at night
And they were creating trumpet sound-

like cry, and was heard at the entire
jungle, sounds of hurting elephants,
sounds of lamentation.
People that were there witnessed
The pouring of the herds' tears,
Do they have emotions? Yes!
Are they grieving? Certainly yes!

Virtues: Be kind to animals, pets and mammals. Elephant is one of the animals at Noah's ark. Lamenting is a healthy way of grieving.

THE PARABLE OF HUMILITY

In the forest near-by there are two trees talking
One is straight up and standing tall,
The other is short and full of leaves.
They look odd standing side by side
But they get along and always share
Their ideas and opinions.
One day the short tree asked the tall tree
"Why is it that you can bend as low as you can?"
"Aren't you hurt reaching the ground?"
The tall tree responded," Yes, it hurts,
But reaching the ground makes me feel good
Bowing down makes me talk to you better
Bending lower I can see you clearer;
And doing all these makes me bigger inside me
Why can't we be like the tall tree,
the role model of humility?

Virtues: Humility…No matter how tall you are, or how rich you are, learn to bow down and reach the poor people. Extend extra help to others. Give extra effort to be humble.

THE PARABLE OF WONDERS

A group of ants gather in a small cave
To talk about the problem they have
The problem is that, they would be
Soon evicted out of the molehill they built.
This group of ants started to move out
Each carries a piece of crumbs
In their mouth
Every time they cross ways, they
Whisper or maybe kiss each other.
Have you ever thought what they're
Talking about?
Does it mean affection and compassion?
Does it mean a warning of upcoming danger?
Or is it a ritual that they practice?
Or is it one of GOD's wonder of wonders?
Yes it is, so don't wonder why?

Virtues: Be observant. Even in little creatures, GOD shows His wonderful deeds. When you get the chance, try to observe the ants' behavior.

THE PARABLE OF COMMON SENSE

A giraffe and a monkey went out for a date.
They had breakfast at the near-by coffee house.
After ordering their breakfast, the monkey went
to the counter at the corner to get hot water for
her tea, (from the thermos.)
Since, she is not that tall, the hot water splatters
on her face. So both of them approached the
manager to suggest to move the thermos with
hot water to where the coffee thermos are. The
manager didn't pay attention to their suggestion.
So they put it in writing and placed it in the suggestion box.

After few months, the giraffe and the monkey
went for a breakfast again in the same coffee
house. Guess what? The thermos with hot water
is already in lined where the coffee thermos are.
Now, every short adult customer can reach the
hot water thermos. And we have two satisfied
customers. Is it true that customer is always right?

*Virtues: Sometimes common sense can help avoid accidents. . Be assertive,
in a tactful way. Be open to suggestions.*

THE PARABLE OF KINDNESS

One Sunday, the animals in the jungle were
celebrating the freedom day. In their minds,
they were thinking of "No Poachers" on Sunday,
so it is a day to celebrate. In the middle of their
fellowship, they heard shots at the near distance.
So everyone ran fast as they can. Most of the
animals were able to hide, but there was this
monkey trapped at the edge of the cliff. He was
trying to cross to the other cliff, but he couldn't.
Unfortuantely there were no trees around for him
to swing with. A giraffe saw his struggle, so
he extended his long neck from one cliff to the
other side of the cliff, and the monkey
then crossed between the cliffs and used the
giraffe's neck as the bridge.
Now, everyone is safe. Is this kindness or what? How
many are there of this kind nowadays? (*The Giraffe's
(sympathetic nature?)*)

*Virtues: Again, be kind to animals. Even animals to animals knows how to
be kind. If you can do a lot of Random Act Of Kindness, this world would
be a better world to live in.*

THE PARABLE OF ABUNDANCE

In a small village there's a couple with a dozen
kid. They hardly could cope with the daily needs.
The family is so happy being together. They
always pray before each meal.
The family receives donation once in a while.
Mind you they are very grateful for that chance.
The children are polite and respectful and you
won't hear them complain at all.
Abundance for them is not a material thing but the
richness of their relationship. Abundance is a
nourishment not only of the food, but of the
soul, too So, will you still dwell on your complaints
and grumbles? Be thankful all the time, that is
ABUNDANCE.

*Virtues: Remember, Blessed are the poor… abundance has a deeper meaning,
(richness of heart and soul)*

I hope you learned something from my few parables. I still have some
parables to share, but let us concentrate on the Parables in the New
Testament. I am wondering,… maybe one of the reasons why our
Almighty created the beautiful animals was, for us to learn lessons from
them, too. GOD is the GOD of Wonders.

The Bible is everything, from A to Z, from cover to cover and it is
complete. Even the parables that I formulated were all based on the
Scriptures. Understanding the Scriptures is a pride to keep, because
you can walk with a head up high knowing that our LORD is behind
all these wonderful deeds and we are given the freedom to choose, that
is to be with GOD. It is an overwhelming feeling just to fathom the
abundance of gifts that I am receiving- (the simplicity of my life, the
knowledge and wisdom that I am utilizing, the values of my faculties
that I am using in an artisitic way, especially my heart, mind and soul;

the shaping of my life through the virtues that were lent to me, and most of all, my relationship with JESUS, my Creator and Savior and the love of our Blessed Mother Mary, not to forget, the invocations of all the Saints and the guarding of my angel constantly.)

Where and when did these things start to be parts of my life? When I started reading the Bible and understanding it in a holy way.

CHAPTER VIII

Inspirational Poems

As the title of the book says, "Deep Inner Thoughts, Concept Of Death, Overcoming Fear, has indeed a lot to say. It portrays sadness, challenge, confession and glory. It is an accumulation of deeper thoughts that needed to be expressed. Ecclesiastically speaking, there is a time to share sadness, sorrows and this time gladness and smiley moments. This time I would like to break the monotony of feeling sentimental, emotional, and even social. All the inspirational poems that you will read next are excerpt from my two books, "What's In My Heart? Volume I and Volume II.

I will start with this poem: "Keeping In Touch." We sometimes fail to acknowledge that we have relatives or friends who needed us or vice versa. All we need is (KIT) Keeping In Touch.

Keeping In Touch

We are busy in our lives, working daily in our job
We don't have time to do extra things
We ignore the vital links
We have our relatives afar, we have our friends near
We have our time to keep in touch
But we didn't even bother.
Keeping in touch is a Christian way
To show someone that you care
To give a ring to say hello
To drop a line and follow through.

Keeping in touch is a reality
It is a reality of Divine Existence of
CHRIST JESUS and GOD's Presence
And this is the reality that makes sense
So let us start keeping in touch
With our loved ones, friends near or far
Because we are spiritually bonded and
Guided by the Holy Spirit, our Advocate
Keeping in touch is one way to keep us
Updated with our kinship and friends
It is one way to extend our service to be
Good listeners and for just being there
Let us keep in touch not only with the people
But with the Best Connector, our Creator.
We have to reach Him whatever it takes
Because He is not only our Creator but
Our Savior.
Keep in touch, remember GOD is within
and between us.

Lately, I have been reviewing my two books, that's why I got the chance to select the ones that would be appropriate for this chapter. Re-reading the inspirational poems helps me in my coping too. Time is really essential. So, let's see how these following poems affect you.

TIME IS GOLD

We are given certain time to live in this world
We are to use our time wisely for whatever its worth
We have to do things, scheduled or not
We should know the value of time because time is gold.
Time is what we have, time is what we need, to
Accomplish our goals to the maximum, to live our
Lives to the fullest, to live up with the expectation
Of the people around us and the nation.

We can only do the best we can and live one day
At a time, as the plan
GOD Has plan for everyone in each clan
Everyone has a map of life to run
When GOD created the world and mankind
He didn't waste time; in six days the creation
Was completed and on the seventh day,
He finally rested and was pleased for what He did.
Time is so precious, so let us think and ponder
On how to make use of our time here and there.
Time is given to us to serve GOD in any ways
So let us grab the chance to tender our service
With honor and grace
Golden moments, must be reassured,
for again TIME IS GOLD.

What do we have in our possession to be worthy of living? Actually, it's not the material possession that I am talking about, but TIME. All we need is TIME, time for everything. The Book of Ecclesiastes says a lot about time. It is essential to acknowledge that without TIME, the world is a chaos.

The following poem is a reminder for us that we have to place ourselves where we can utilize our precious time.

"A TICK OF TIME"

This is based on *Ecclesiastes 3:2 and 4, a time to be born and a time to die, a time to plant, and a time to uproot the the plant. A time to weep and a time to laugh; a time to mourn, and a time to dance.*
Time is essential, time is demanded,
Time is the gauge in this revolving earth
You see a new born babe, you witness
death; You feel the joy in your heart
After your moments of hurt, there are

moments of tears there are moments of
laughters, there are moments of silence
And moments to converse.
Life is too short to do all the things
We wanted in life but we can only
Do our best to the fullest
For a "tick of time"is just a click
Of a life's moment.

In order for us to be reassured of Heaven or going to the Pathway to Heaven, we have to invest good deeds on earth. It is not easy to do the right thing or to be righteous. In other words to straighten our lives is a long process. One of the things we needed to do is to start with something. Maybe this following poem could help.

TAME OUR TONGUE

Often times we say things that are hurtful
Deep in our hearts we are regretful
Amending mistakes is commendable
Let's tame our tongue, we need to do more.
Let us guard our thoughts and ask for that grace
Let's ask the Holy Spirit's guidance
Let's think more than once what to say and
Let's tame our tongue, or bite it if you can
A tongue can be sharp and can be polite
A tongue can cut and can love
We have the choice of what we want
Let's be aware and vigilant
And just focus on something nice and
Pleasant, for GOD is the Best Tamer of
all mankind.

One thing sure in my life nowadays is I am learning to be detached bit by bit from the materialistic world. I am less vain now through the help of the Holy Spirit. Detachment is difficult to do but with the help of the divine intervention and the power of prayer, we can attain the simple life that our LORD would like us to have. He will let us realize that we cannot take our vanities to Heaven. So instead of tolerating our vanities in life, let us detach ourselves from the things that we are attached to, from being too dependent on unpleasant relationship; from drug addictions and different vices. Think of your own attachments and gradually detach yourselves from them. Let's pray about it. Here's a poem that might guide us in our detachment.

DETACHMENT

Vanity of vanities, you are so tempting
You give us pleasure and you're so soothing
We're engrossed with material things and
enjoy our lives
But we almost forget, they are ony materials
We buy this and we buy that, we treasure the
luxury, we dwell on the wealth
We spend lavishly and throw a bunch of waste
Let's make a change and go for detachment
We gain more not in wealth but in health.
Not only in materials are we so attached
Even in a relationship and situation as well
We need the grace from GOD to live in norm
The norm to be humble and spend no more.
Detachment is difficult to do
But if we ask GOD's grace we'll be able to
So start listing your attachments
And convert them to detachments.
We can start to have a simple life
And be satisfied with what we have
Just think of the unfortunate people
Who lives on one meal a day, and no home at all.
One thing sure is guaranteed here on earth
Is we won't be able to carry anything upstairs
The upstairs I meant is the heavenly kingdom

That is waiting for us, our spiritual advancement.
O LORD our GOD continue to guide us
In our spiritual struggle with our detachment
We want to be attached with You alone
Thank You for our spiritual conversion.

We can't escape death, there's no tunnel of escape. Death is just around the corner. It comes by surprise, unexpected and sometimes no warning at all.

This book is about preparation too. Be ready and be prepared at all times. Mind you, it pays. It is very unfortunate for the victims of sudden death. I am referring to the incident happened, last week, (January 25,2015) when we lost 44 police officers, (the PNP SAF) Philippine National Police Special Action Force. My prayers are for the victims and the bereaved. I believe there was no chance to prepare for their death, so both the victims and the mourners were not able to prepare their hearts and minds for the unexpected "silent thief". My facing of the uncertainties of death makes me more courageous. Death is like a thief that comes surprisingly.

Allow me to share with you another poem that I wrote entitled "The Silent Thief"

THE SILENT THIEF

In the middle of the night it comes to you
You're not aware the silent thief is there
You are in a party enjoying your time
You suddenly collapse, the silent thief reacts
You are in the hospital as a patient
You're only for check-up, guess who is there?
"The Silent Thief"
You're above 80 years old,
You are a newly born
You're at the height of your success

The silent thief makes the selection
Maybe by now you know what I am
talking about?
It's the mysterious death known in ages
Death may come upon us like a thief
in the night and launch us into eternal
present; we can't beat death and there
is no antidote.
But we can have a brighter outlook
That is, we should always be prepared
Like the way we prepare for the second
coming of the LORD JESUS.
The silent thief we shouldn't be scared
Just trust everything to GOD even our
Death; He will help us to prepare by any
Means including being a friend with a
Silent thief.
So let us have peace in our hearts and minds.
Be prepared as in the Boy Scout's creed.
Please LORD just be with us every step of
The way and any moment.

How often in your life do you receive praises and how often do you praise someone? If you have the chance to praise someone would you do it? How are you when it comes to saying, 'I'm sorry', how about "I love you?"

It is important to have a better communication in any relationship. Some of the ways to have better communication are to be open, to be assertive and to be keen observer. These are means of investing good deeds on earth. Another essential thing is don't procrastinate The time is NOW. It's never too late to initiate. Here is an elaboration of the two poems, "The Now" and the other is "It's Never Too Late."

THE NOW

"Live one day at a time", our motto should be in life
Think of now and never to dwell on yesterday
Be better today than yesterday, Be better tomorrow
than today, do the best you can and make the most
of it; You can glance at the rear view mirror, when
you're driving a car, and it means you can only
recall your past from time to time.
If you want to change for better, you should do
it now or never, and grab the chance without
hesitation. Opportunity knocks only once in a while
Memories are not current ; Live not in memories,
live in now; You don't know what's in for tomorrow,
Tomorrow might never come, you can plan ahead
for the whole year but GOD Has plans for everyone
Including the now.
So be healthy now and live wisely, serve humanity,
serve your family, and serve the LORD most of all.
Whatever you do today is rewarding because you
are working on your sturdy future.
The future is tomorrow, the past is yesterday
Whatever you say, do and think now
Do it to the fullest; Be at peace with everyone, with
yourself and with our Creator; He will show you
the way to NOW and here, then to eternity.

It's never too late to do the things you want to do now. We love to procrastinate. And the (Manana habit which is pronounced as) "Maniana Habit" is glued in our body. The term "maniana" means tomorrow and this habit of I'll do it tomorrow was adapted from the Spaniards, during the Spanish colonization of our country. We can avoid the maniana habit, if we want to. It's never too late to accomplish the things you want to accomplish. So, let's break the habit of "I'll do it tomorrow". One advantage of being on the go all the time is, you are clearing things, sweeping the obstacles that cross your way. And what does this mean? It means it is also clearing your conscience. Allow me to be heavy a little bit in my sharing of point of view. How about going for confession? It's never too late. Ponder on this.

Here is a poem that would guide us on what to do now instead of tomorrow.

IT'S NEVER TOO LATE.

It's time to start now saying "I love you mom,"
"I love you dad", I love you all".
Well done, that's good.
But let's think and ponder whom we've hurt
It's time to say, "I'm sorry, please forgive me?"
Wait a minute, how about us?
Can we forgive too? Now?
In my heart and in my thoughts
I forgive you; I forgive those who
Have hurt me, persecute, condemn
And humiliate me
I'll call someone now to say, "hello"
to say, "I'm thinking of you",
I'll write a short note to a friend
Or I'll visit a relative in the hospital
I'll serve in the community
Am I too late, but, don't wait too long
Time can wait, chances cannot
Time to start to make amends,
to reconcile, to get in touch with
our loved ones.
There'll be peace, joy and contentment
as the ultimate reward
Can I write You LORD a note, a letter of
gratitude, or can I call You from my heart?
I won't wait up to the last moment

IT'S NEVER TOO LATE!
*What are you waiting for? Do it now
and say it now, it's not too late my
dear readers.*

There are three phrases that are essential for better communication and for better relationship. They are: "I am sorry", "I thank you" and "I love you." These are words of gratitude. We should cultivate the attitude of gratitude. This attitude is not only for Thanksgiving Day but for everyday.

THE ATTITUDE OF GRATITUDE

There is a time for everything
A time for everyone
A time to say "thank you"
For whatever GOD Has done
We thank you LORD for everyday
For the abundance that You share
For the protection You have granted
For Your love, mercy and care
We are thankful and grateful O LORD
For the Holy Spirit's gifts
The gift of life
The gift of family
The gift of friendship
The gift of community

On November, we celebrate Thanksgiving Day, please allow us to offer our prayers of gratitude. In You we lift up all our problems and concerns. Without Your grace we are indebted forever. Thanksgiving or not, we thank You all year through, for without You we are nothing, we ask You LORD to grant us the grace of "Attitude of Gratitude" in all circumstances.

There are many things in this world that we can do to make use of our quality time. Again, I will say this,"Life is too Short," and what are we going to do with the time given to us? One of the things that we are privilege to do is, the freedom to choose. We can choose between good or bad, to be happy or sad, to say yes or no, or to a more complicated situation as to judge guilty or not guilty and to choose between virtues or vices. I think the latter are choices of how to use our time.We can be lavished (if we have the means) and can spend our money to gamble, to get drunk, and even to use legal drugs. On the other hand, you can gather a lot of virtues from respectable people or you can be involved in a charity organization and have the heart to donate something to the needy. For the simple things you can practice The "Random Act Of Kindness." Another noble thing is serving the community and this is one great choice. Maybe you need time to ponder on this. I have a poem for us to ponder.

A DESIRE TO SERVE

Willingness, spoken from the heart
Servanthood the way it must
A call to serve, a desire I have
Ministry of service let me accept.
Life is too short wanting **a quality life**
To serve humanity like our CHRIST JESUS
Fulfillment and rewards are great feelings
Guided by the Holy Spirit with everything.
Our LORD Almighty thank You for the chance
The chance to offer my moments of life
To work on Your plans feeding Your lambs
To serve You my LORD, my sincere desire.
Serving You is my delight
Please lead my heart where it demands
May it be with the elders or with the youth
Yes my LORD my service I'll offer with all
My heart.
Yes! My LORD, I have a desire to serve You

I am offering myself and everything I do
I need Your grace LORD all the way through
I need Your love and mercy, I really do
Bless me LORD and I bless You too.

Have you ever heard GOD's voice? Of course no one would seriously say, they did. The answer might be yes or no. Yes, we can hear GOD's voice through our heart. It isn't exactly the sound of a voice, but the power of the Holy Spirit. The Holy Spirit empowers us by allowing us to feel the Presence of GOD.

Spiritually speaking, the messages are still received and in the following poem, you'll know its essence. The poem is self explanatory and the messages are very clear...that GOD is communicating with us and talking to us. He is allowing us to be aware of His Presence. So, let us hear GOD's messages and listen to His voice that can be only heard through our hearts. The Holy Spirit is giving us a listening heart.

DEAFENED HEART

I am calling you by name
I am waiting for you to come
I can be patient, I have time
I, your LORD, is knocking at your
Deafened heart.
My voice I let you hear
The whispering that I do
Remained Unnoticed
You seemed so occupied and busy
Obviously you didn't hear me
With your deafened heart
I am here for you everyday
I just want you to listen and
Open your heart
You woke up in the middle of the

Night, you said you heard my voice
Then you started to pray and called
My name; You claimed you felt
My Presence.
I led you the way to a place so quiet
I let you feel the peace in your heart
I told you I was going to wait
I know that your heart is temporarily deaf
The sound of my voice you finally heard
It echoed inside your deafened heart,
The loudness of my call penetrates your
being, deaf no more and now you can hear
It's Me that you feel
I bless you my child for you no longer
Have a deafened heart.

*Every poem that is selected to be in this book pertains on"what to do with
your time while you're still on earth. How would you spend the valuable
moments you have? What are the means of support you'll utilize to have
quality life? There are more to these querries. But the bottom line is, let
us invest good deeds and plant fertile seeds while we have time on earth.
Pondering on all the poems written here would help us realize the essence
of relationship, the value of life, the cultivation of virtues and anything that
would smoothen the rough edges in this chaotic world. In the poem below,
it says, "if we have compassion, we can change the world.*

COMPASSION

A genuine heart must you possess
To tame an angry human being
A soft touch with caring thoughts
And with a tender, loving care
Compassion, a beautiful virtue to aim
You can start now and learn from it
It's an amulet for a raging bull

And a shield to protect you with
With a caring hand and a smiling face
With a friendly gesture of shaking hands
With gentle words to the listening ears
And that is the meaning of "compassion."
So be compassionate and be friendly
You will see the big change yourself
You didn't change the people, they changed you
You change the world, that is compassion.

"Prayers can move mountains," as the adage says. Prayers are powerful when accompanied by strong faith and belief. Miracles happen. If you want to change for the better, you just need to pray for it and pray about it.

Try to read it slowly and loud and feel it and you'll see in the mirror the miracle and the miracle is you.

SEE THROUGH MY SOUL

I see the beauty of life when I wake up in the morning
I see hope when I look up the sky, I see the miracle of life
When I look at the mirror
Yes, you can see my true self through my soul.
I see us the people of many faces
I see the wonderful talents in each one
I see how beautiful we are created in GOD's Image
Indeed, I am thankful for my sight and all my senses
I am grateful for all my blessings and graces
I am blessed with loving family and great friends
You can see through my soul, the fullness of my gratitude
Yes, GOD can see me through
my very being, through my soul.

Since we've been talking and discussing the uncertainties of death, the gift of life, and my own major issues of reality decision, there's a closer relationship in the next poem. It is describing the close affinity of life and death, almost kissing each other. Let's see how essential it is to know the reality of miracle and mystery.

BIRTH VS. DEATH

From womb to tomb, the life span
New life comes into the world
The gift of life freely given
The miracle happens, it's amazing
Growth processes, development starts
Environment takes a big part in the
Growing process of life
Family involvement is also important
You can ask yourself What's the use of life?
We're born in this world to die In the
long run. Birth and death are compatible
There is a specific time for each one
Welcome into this world for birth
Good-bye from the earth for death
Enjoy the gift of life that GOD Has given
But let us prepare our way to Heaven
The miracle of life, the mystery of death
Both are included in GOD's great plans.

This is the conclusion of this chapter. I am glad that I am able to select appropriate poems for this chapter. At least there are variations of theme, but the bottom line is they are all inspirational.

This last inspirational poem is about contentment, satisfaction, and peace, that Our Blessed Mother is imparting to us and because it tells about the utmost and ultimate hope of mankind. Through her intercession, we are reassured of God's true love for us.

OUR MOTHER, THE BLESSED

How awesome just to know you're there
How peaceful my mind is, feeling your warmth
How great the Holy Spirit, generous with His gifts
The gift I received, the love of our Mother,
the Blessed
Our Mother, thank you for aiding me in
my daily life
For interceding in my every strife;
The love and care that you extend
The help we need, you do can sense
Our Mother, can I call my mother?
"Yes my dear child", your holy answer
I feel secured now and in every moment
because I know what my heart says,
"You are loved by your mother isn't it great?
When I pray the "Hail Mary" the fullness
of your grace I feel,
The assurance that the LORD is with Thee
My weapon in this world I see
You bless among the rest of the world
the women you behold, the fruit that you
bear, the Savior of us all.
Oh my Holy Mother of GOD, thank you
For praying for us not only for our needs
but also for our great sins
You love us now and even to the time
Of our last moments
I love you my dear Mother and bless us
Now and forever, Amen!

Our Blessed Virgin Mary, is letting us know the following, with full reassurance: That…GOD is bigger than any problems, GOD is the only

One who can love us unconditionally, GOD is everywhere and will be there waiting for us in Heaven.

If you think that GOD IS <u>NO WHERE</u>…JUST MOVE A LITTLE

And see what happens…GOD IS <u>NOW HERE!</u>

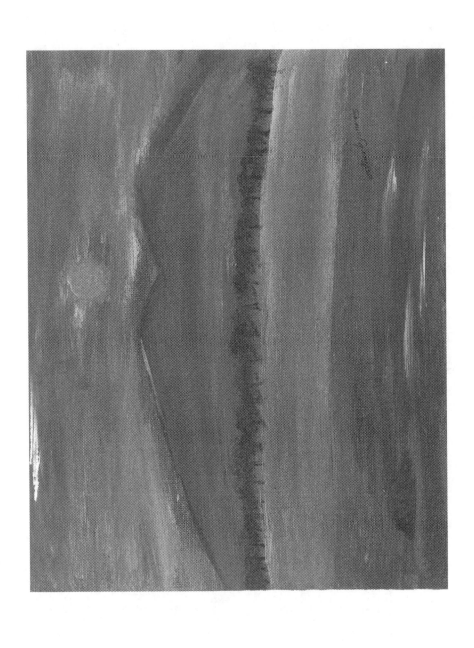

CHAPTER IX

My Conversation With God

I believe that the best prayer is to commune with GOD. Our GOD listens to our plea, to all the things we say to Him and even to our complaints. He acknowledges our prayers, may they be silent or vocal ones. He talks to our hearts and consoles our being. What GOD wants is, to listen to Him and to feel His Presence. And this is really how to have a conversation with GOD. It is more on listening through our hearts and focusing on what He wants to convey to us. GOD's messages for us are very clear. He would like us to ponder and to utilize the wisdom that He imparted to us.

Let us have a quality time with GOD and talk to Him. Let me walk you to the valley of the Word, the LORD Almighty Himself and let us witness the healing power just by conversing with Him.

The truth is, this whole book is already my conversation with GOD. My deep inner thoughts are coming from my heart and slowly flowing through my blood until they reach my vocal cords to speak of them, commanding my hands and fingers to do the walking up to the finishing line of my book.

After pouring out my concerns, after my final discernment and after the ten chapters that I tackled, I would like to conclude the totality of my inner thoughts after all the chapters. They say that the equivalent of one minute to GOD is a lot of years for us. So, a minute with GOD is our chance of years to show GOD how much we love Him, a chance of years to cultivate virtues and a chance of years to do good. How about sharing with you a poem entitled," A Minute With GOD.?"

A MINUTE WITH GOD

Do you have a minute with GOD?
Just to say, "Hello LORD how are you today?"
Or just to say, "Thank You LORD, I am alive
For another day
Or just to take a deep breath and feel
The life in you
Or just to close your eyes and whisper,
"LORD, I love you"
Do you have a minute with GOD, to feel
His Presence in this chaotic world, to
Appreciate His creations and creatures
And more so of nature,
Do you have a minute to nod your head
And smile in secret to let Him know you're
Happy, you are created in His Image?
A minute with GOD, a minute to love
A minute to love is a minute
Of peace, a minute of peace is GOD's
Reward for the time you spent to show
Your love, so, do you have a minute with GOD?

Have you ever experienced a long conversation with our LORD? I did. I find solace, peace and contentment talking to GOD. There's a delight in my heart every time I spend my moments in front of the Blessed Sacrament. The key to a fruitful conversation with GOD is, learn to listen and have moments of silence with Him. That's the conversation that GOD wants, that is talking to Him with our hearts. So pray with that listening heart.

Part of what I do whenever I am in my adoration is, I always say all the mysteries of the rosary. Another thing is, I have this rosary called"2000 Hail Marys", in which I say one hundred beads of Hail Mary a day for 20 days. So a total of 2,000 Hail Marys in a month. I am doing this every first day of every month up to the 20th day of the same month. I have been doing this for almost seven years now. There is a petition mentioned for everyday,including adoration,contrition, thanksgiving and supplication. Sometimes I stay in front of the Blessed Sacrament for at least 2-4 hours. I am overwhelmed to share that, it's rewarding to have a conversation with GOD. *LORD, the following apportioned sharing are my inner thoughts regarding the contents of this book. I would just randomly pour them out to You my LORD.*

Behind my fears and uncertainties is You my LORD CHRIST JESUS. You are with me in my every move. You are there in my sorrow, sadness, and suffering, even in my unpleasant moods. So, I am moving on with the assurance of Your compassion LORD, You are my Greatest Companion.

I have more inner thoughts to share.

This I can say, whatever the number of population here on this earth, that is the number of ways to die. No two ways to die is alike. We should remember that we are just temporary inhabitants in this world.There is no such permanency.We just borrowed our life from our Creator. Our time is limited. Nobody is guaranteed to live forever. I am emphasizing the reality of facing death here.

Morbidity aside, I am aware of the consequences that early detection will prevent the early occurrence of malignancy and occurrence of sooner death. You see, death can happen soon or can be delayed, that's it. The most important thing is what would you do before that occurrence?

LORD, I am not giving facts and informations about things to influence the minds of the readers I am extracting what I am saying from my heart and mind. Shall I go on LORD? I have more to share.

In 2 Corinthians 5:10, it says,"*For all of us must appear before CHRIST, to be judged by Him. Each one will receive what he deserves, according to everything he has done, good or bad in his bodily life.*"

I believe that JESUS is LORD and this is one of the reasons why my faith is getting stronger and stronger. Whatever and however we stand on earth, is the gauge in going to Heaven. When we reach the gate of heaven, we'll be facing the Holy people with dignity and humility.

This is one of the main reasons why I am building up my confidence in whatever I do especially my decision of not having mammogram done. *LORD, whenever I feel the pain on my breast, I sometimes cry hard, sometimes I shout and I end up saying,"LORD, I love you, take good care of my soul." Grant me Your love and mercy."*

Once in a while I am throwing some lines to my cousin like, "I want you to continue to pray for me and my soul." And in a jokingly manner, I would add "Take good care of Pong," (my real pet turtle.) I also am expressing what I want when I die. I told her that I do not want "cremation." I even mentioned about the music that I wanted to be played, and that is "Air On The G-String played by Gheorge Zamfir, a flute player. Sometimes, it seems silly hearing what I am saying, but I didn't even know that such boldness came out from my mouth.

*LORD, please don't tell me that I am becoming silly. I hope my (tidbits) confession don't bore you. I know LORD, You are a good listener. Thank You for Your patience. I am grateful LORD that I reached this age of sixty-seven. I don't have any regrets at all knowing I had a good life, have a good life, and would continue to have a good life, and **a quality life.***

What is **a quality life?** For me, it is being aware of what to do and what to say, and being aware of what is right and what is wrong. **Quality of life** is always thinking that today or everyday is our last day. If we are aware that today is our last day, we would be aware of our words and actions, meaning taming our tongues, guiding our thoughts and guarding our actions. Again, let's be aware of the present and deal with the present in a holy way. This is the best investment on earth and the profit is a place called,"Heaven."

LORD, I am glad that You have given me the gift of awareness. I have never been conscious of what I say and do until the time my life was transformed, more so now that I am working my way up to "Heaven."

Heaven is real, according to Colton, (the little boy in the book, Heaven Is For Real.) *After reading this book and saw this in a movie, I am very much convinced the reality of Heaven. I already knew that Heaven is real, but this book enhanced my belief. LORD, the most inspiring encounter of this little boy Colton while he was in Heaven, was, when he met Your Son, JESUS. He even described Him when he came back to earth. It is reassuring LORD that You are using people like Colton, to reveal that there is Heaven.*

Let us all work on our way up because Heaven Can Wait.

I have many reasons why I am so bold now in facing the uncertainties of death. One of them is my feeling of being reassured that I am going to a better place called "Heaven." Yes, the word is reassurance. Isn't it that if somebody reassure you of something positive and pleasant you will feel at ease and at peace? I think it is almost the same as a "promise." GOD fulfills His promises. Yes, I have the same feeling of peace and at ease, knowing that there is Someone Who is watching over me and even waiting for me, letting me feel that everything will be taken cared of by Him, the Almighty.

Yes, this is one of the many reasons why I feel confident with my decision (especially) the one about undergoing a mammogram.

I really have a lot of thoughts to share and my heart would like to let those thoughts out. Instead of grouping my thoughts into more chapters, the Holy Spirit indeed led me to suggest a better way to include such thoughts in my book.

While I am finishing this book, this idea of the Holy Spirit pops in. I was on the 9th chapter which is " My Conversation With GOD" when I thought of this idea. Since I still have more (inner thoughts) to share, I wanted to name these thoughts(inner thoughts tidbits.)

I would still continue my conversation with GOD and offer Him the rest of my inner thoughts.

So, LORD can I continue my conversation with You? Please bear with me my Almighty for I would be jumping from one thought to another. You see LORD, everytime I am in my solitude, thoughts come and go and I couldn't help but write them. In my many solitudes, there are more thoughts that I need to share, my LORD. So can I start now with one of my inner thought tidbits?

While I was finishing this manuscript, I ran across the word "myalgia". Being a nurse, I am familiar with it. I know it is a muscle pain. I remember that the breasts are tissues that are overlying the chest muscles. So, I googled about it and I ran across another term "mastalgia", which means breasts' pain. Upon knowing about it I was a bit relieved. Now, my breasts would have a little freedom to be safer with muscle pain rather than with cancerous gain (cancer cells). Whether cancer or mastalgia, my thoughts and my discern- ment stands the same, no mammogram nor biopsy, no chemotherapy nor radiation.

Our mind is so powerful. And I believed that being a positive thinker is a virtue. I aimed to have this kind of virtue, that is to be a positive thinker in dealing with my deep inner thoughts. Instead of baby sitting my old ways of dealing with my fears and worries, I am engrossed on how I can function normally.

I will say it again, I wanted **a quality life.** That's one of the main reasons why I have this book. Each chapter of this book, will help us understand the essence of wanting to live and facing death fearlessly.

LORD, I am indeed being led by the Holy Spirit. I was led to find out the terms such as myalgia and mastalgia. Instead of the word,"cancer", it is now "just" mastalgia. This is what I'm saying to myself ...I'll be open and I will allow the Holy Spirit to enter into my heart and will receive the gift of wisdom.

O LORD, how awesome the Holy Spirit is and He is very generous. I can't thank You enough for journeying with me and my book, with the Holy Spirit at my side.

Recently, I had a conversation with a friend of mine who asked me if I already had a flu shot or any of the shots recommended. I told her that I didn't have any of the shots, because I am hypersensitive and I am allergic to immunization shots. During our conversation, I had the chance to ask her too, if she had a mammogram recently. I was surprised when she said, "Never". So, I asked her why. She started saying, "It never occurred to me to go for a mammogram. And I really didn't want to. If I die, I'll die. With or with out cancer, we'll die anyway."

I didn't comment anymore. Honestly, I felt at ease not because we are on the same boat, but I felt good because I am not alone. At least for me I have experienced to undergo mammogram. Actually, I should not brag about that, because the point here is the now, the present time and the **quality of life.** I am only talking about my opinion here. Well, what can I do? That's how I feel. I am just being honest, true to myself and to others. Anyway, I also knew few more friends of mine who are scared to have a mammogram. Whatever the reasons of my friends are, I have nothing to do with their decisions.

*LORD, I am not thrilled nor happy knowing a few people, including some friends who didn't want to go for mammogram nor don't want to go for it. I know LORD that the Holy Spirit is with them, too. LORD, let me reiterate that I would like to have **a quality life** and wanted to function normally and wanted to focus on good things. Most of all LORD, I wanted to serve You in a fruitful way, a productive one. These are enough reasons of my disinterest to have mammogram nor biopsy. I will say it again, I am not campaigning for saying "no" to mammogram nor refraining from any diagnostic procedure for women. This book is purely my concept, my discernment and my wanting to have **a quality life.** Opinions differ, but instead of opposing each other, we can make the difference and should celebrate our differences by knowing that we are spiritual beings sharing a* *common physical experience. Our differences lead us to our commonality which is we are interconnected in the tapestry called life. Through the cycle of life and death and rebirth, we learn who we are and why we are here. Opinions should be respected.*

Heavenly Father, I am adamant with my way of serving You. I am adamant with my decisions regarding my thoughts. I need a real quality time to pray longer, fervently, and focused. So, LORD allow me to verbalize all my concerns and I beg for Your understanding, all the time. This entails the normality of my life. Normality includes the strength that I need especially the strength of praying and this is one of the utmost reasons why I am adamant with my decision. For me, praying in a normal state of mind is clearer, focused and more time spent. When I say more time spent, I meant praying longer and the intercessory is also longer.

When you are not in a normal state of mind and you are focused on your pains and discomfort, where will the quality of prayer goes? The bottom line is, it is between you and GOD. Sometimes doing the sign of the cross has a meaningful effect and GOD understands where we stand.

Before I go on, I would like to request the readers to imagine a person undergoing chemotherapy. I am not going to describe how it is to be in this situation. This particular issue is just about me and my opinion. I do not want to be in that situation. I want to be untouched or unattached from the gadget of chemical treatment and radiation. Again, this is me. I apologize if I have offended those women undergoing treatment. Actually, this is my body I am talking about; it is my service that I am fulfilling of, it is my way of life wanting **a quality life**.

LORD GOD, please take good care of my spirituality.

If cancer is popular, it is equally popular with chemotherapy or radiation. I agree that if a woman is diagnosed early and would submit for the recommended treatment such as chemotherapy or radiation, there would be a chance of additional years of survival. But I also have witnessed that in some cases, that, right after the mammogram, they would hear the words"Stage IV", you have so and so months to live. So we cannot be sure at all, where someone stands in this breast's cancer business.

So, with my fervent prayers and with the Holy Spirit's guidance, I chose the pathway road to **a quality of life**.

I do not have anything against the diagnostic procedure and treatment for cancer of any kind. As a matter of fact I am for it, especially for early detection. I respect very much the cancer survivors, patients undergoing chemotherapy or radiation, and women submitting for yearly breast check-up and mammogram.

Whatever you read in this book, they are purely my own prerogative, my own thoughts, my fate, my beliefs and my principles.

There is a support group for the pre and post chemotherapy or radiation for cancer patients. There is no support group for a circle of women, who don't want to go for breast exam and mammogram. But I am aware that there are a lot of women who are in the same situation like me. Well, the most essential factor in dealing with my own situation is my hope and faith for a better future, better place to go without fear of the unknown.

In 2 Peter 3:15, it says," *And consider the patience of our LORD as salvation, as our beloved brother Paul, according to the wisdom given to him, also wrote to you.*"

Paul was given wisdom by GOD and if he was given this gift, definitely everyone whom He created would receive the same treatment and of course we have to pray and ask for it. I thank the Holy Spirit for the gift of wisdom and knowledge. I strongly believe that whatever you do in life always pray for it and pray about it. And when you do this, GOD will give you the gift of understanding and the gift of wisdom.

Saying good-byes is a two way process. Most of the time, when we talk about saying good-bye, it is the ones being left who suffer, feel the sorrow and has difficulty of facing the reality of their loss. Learning to say good-bye is the start of grieving. My purpose of mentioning about this good-bye business is for the one saying good-bye to the mourners.

But right now, the difference (in what I am going to say) is no one is dead here and yet there is a good-bye to discuss about. I'm referring to the theme of this book, my own confession, and my inner thoughts. This is it…my own good-bye, my facing of the uncertainties of death, my morbid, but realistic thought. I don't need to elaborate in this page about the topic of good-bye…because this is me, on how I'll bid adieu, when my time is due.

My LORD, I have this wish of mine about saying good-byes. I wished that I would be the last person to die. Why? I don't want my loved ones to feel the hurt. It hurts when you lose someone you love. I would like to carry on their burden of mourning. Thank You my LORD for the gift of humility and gift of prayer.

No one knows who leaves this earth and when, whether me first, or me last. I really offer my prayers for the spiritual strength and tenacity for every mourners and everyone concerned. So LORD Bless us all forever.

Let us see how our LORD JESUS handle His remaining time in this world. In John 13:1 it says *"Before the feast of Passover, JESUS knew that his hour had come to pass from this world to the Father. He loved his own in the world and he loved to the end"*. He thought of His disciples right away. He showed his obedience and humility by accepting the coming of His death. JESUS faced the consequences of everything including the primary, major and even the ultimate mission of ransoming our sins. One thing sure is, as a human being JESUS was sweating profusely and very anxious few hours before he was summoned by the Roman soldiers.

LORD GOD Almighty, Your Son JESUS is true to His promise and He fulfills everything within the span of time, the time allotted to Him. When

Your Son JESUS asked the disciples to spend an hour to watch Him at the Gethsemane, that was the start of His unconditional, tremendous and awesome love for mankind. That was the start of the Agony of CHRIST JESUS followed by the Passion of CHRIST.

LORD GOD, I will not end this chapter without conversing with You and without receiving your closure blessing of my book. Again, my LORD, thank You for allowing me to talk to You, pouring out everything that I needed to express. Thank You for listening to my tidbits' stories about the contents of my book., and the scope of my being human. Please shift my humanity to divinity so I can truly and sincerely work on my way to HEAVEN.

In Philippians 3:20,21 it says,"But our citizenship is in heaven, and it is from there that we are expecting a Savior, the LORD JESUS CHRIST. He will transform the body of our humiliation, that it may be conformed to the body of his glory, by the power that also enbles him to make all things subject to himself.

LORD, GOD, Almighty I am inclined to respond to one of your Bible verses. I just came from the church and I kept thinking how I can express my desire to put all the chapters in one Scriptural message. I just don't want to write the Bible verse, but to say more to give meaning to what my book is really all about. Thank you for this Bible verse from Psalm 90:12 that says, "Teach us to count our days aright that we may gain wisdom of heart."

The message of the psalmist is for us to appreciate the number of years given to us and to use these years in doing GOD's will. Also we are asked to acquire a correct view of life, to work out our salvation through out our life. And all this is given us in wisdom, which discerns the true values and gives the righteous a realistic attitude according to the divine will.

Even in the Bible, it is clear that GOD is giving us the chance to prepare while we're still alive. He is reminding us that our stay on earth is just a temporary thing. The Bible verse is letting us know that we should give value to every gift that our LORD is giving us. I can't emphasize enough the essence of investing good deeds for our holy pathway to Heaven. Instead of wasting our time with the vanities of life, why don't we spend our time wisely. That's what the Bible is emphasizing, "that we may gain wisdom of heart."

The whole chapters of this book are the results of GOD's given wisdom of heart, to a thankful being like me. Let's start with the <u>Fear Of Dying</u> in which GOD Has given me the gift of faith of facing death graciously. I thank our Almighty for all the prayers that aided me in everything I do. Through prayers, I learned a lot about the title of the book and what this entails. These are the sharing of my <u>Deep Inner Thoughts;</u> the delving of the <u>Concept of Death</u>; and the <u>Overcoming of Fear</u> through my strong faith.

Regarding <u>Eulogy,</u> it is very essential to include it as one of the chapters, to emphasize the honor and respect rendered to the reposed and the bereaved.

With everything that I do on earth I learned to give importance to my life. I value my time. I spend it to invest good deeds, because <u>Life Is Too Short.</u>

Since my book deals with the mysterious death, I can't help not to mention <u>Lamentations,</u> a healthy way to grieve.

I have included <u>Inspirational Insights</u>, so we can cope with our sufferings and pains. Part of the inspirational insights are the <u>Inspirational Poems</u> that are related to the normal routine of life's daily endeavors. All the chapters that are in this book are supported by <u>Understanding Scriptures</u>. Most of all through my constant <u>Conversation With GOD</u>. I feel fully gratified with His Presence. GOD is the Alpha and the Omega of my being. This is the beginning of my enlightenment of what life is realizing the existence of death.

My Epilogue is enough for my soul searching and I found fully the Holy Spirit within me.

Let me reiterate of this Bible verse, Psalm 90:12, "Teach us to count our days aright that we may gain wisdom of heart."

Let me conclude in this part of the book with my saying of these lines, from the Profession of Faith, "He will come again to judge the living and the dead and His Kingdom will have no end."

All I can say is, we are all pilgrims, travelers and visitors on earth. Earth is only our temporary dwelling place. Let us work on our way to the final place where we can feel the equality, justice, holy camaraderie, endless love, unfathomable joy way of life and the everlasting peace of our Almighty and the awaited reunion with our beloved families. This place is our real home and it has a very beautiful name. It is open for business everyday (247) I wish to see a lot of souls getting in. Yes, my dear readers allow me to guide you for this preview of HEAVEN. Over there or up there, in the Great Beyond, in Eternity are angels gathering and waiting for us. Again, Heaven Can Wait…

CHAPTER X

Epilogue

I don't know why I am so adamant finishing my book. As a matter of fact, I feel like rushing as if I'm chasing something or somebody or I am being chased. Maybe, I am rushing for I am chasing the time.

Every time I feel the pain in my breasts, I have the urge to rush a little bit. I want to be honest my dear readers in my sharing. Maybe I am just making sure that my book would be out before our Creator winks at me, giving me signal that I should be ready. They say that a person knows or feels when her/his time is coming. Am I feeling that? To be honest I do not know what I feel and how to deal with what I feel. One thing sure is I strongly feel that I needed to share what I would like to do with the remaining time I have in this world. Morbidity aside, everybody is leaving this earth. It is just a matter of when???

So whether a person will die soon or later he/she has to prepare. I am just bold enough to tackle about it. Denial is in our blood. We live in the real world, where no one and nothing is permanent. It seems like I am setting time for myself. Not really. I am just being boldly practical of the reality of life and death.

After the book has been published and I am still breathing, I'll hold the book up and would shout at the top of my voice, "Thank You my LORD" for delaying Your invitation, for honoring my RSVP which is good for indefinite expiration. Thank You for Your mighty deeds.

Thank You so much my LORD, in our dialect, (Maraming salamat po Panginoon).

To some people, they might think I am a morbid person, that I think of the unthinkable thoughts. You see, I am one of those people who functions according to how I feel. But when I do things I pray for it, and pray about it. I pray for my every move. I wouldn't like to lose my connection with my Creator. I know He is empowering me with His love.

In 2 Timothy 1:7, it says, *"For GOD gave us spirit not of fear but of power and love and self-control." With His power I am reassured of His constant guidance.*

I am not adamant only to finish this book, but adamant to stand for what I believe in, to function normally and feel the **quality of life.** When a professional medical person tells you you have 7 months to live, what would you do? Me? My answer would be, I would continue my already established relationship with GOD. And that's enough for my remaining time. My timetable with GOD is going to be extended up in heaven.

NEHEMIAH gives us a very vivid description of how to live **a quality life.**..It says in Nehemiah 1: 5-9, 5 I said, " O LORD GOD of heaven, the great and awesome GOD who keeps covenant and steadfast love with those who love Him and keep his commandments, 6 let your ear be attentive and your eyes open to hear the prayer of your servant that I now pray before you day and night for your servants, the people of Israel, confessing the sins of the people of Israel, which we have sinned against you. Both I and my family have sinned. 7 We have offended you deeply, failing to keep the commandments, the statutes, and the ordinances that you commanded your servant Moses. 8 Remember that you commanded your servant Moses, "If you are unfaithful, I will scatter you among the peoples, 9 but if you return to me and keep my commandments and do them, though your outcasts are under the farthest skies, I will gather them from there and bring them to the place at which I have chosen to establish my name.

*LORD Almighty, I know it is very difficult to attain **a quality life,** but through your constant guidance and reminder I know I would be able to pull it through. I am blessed with the Holy Spirit who constanly tapping me at my back and helping me to use my faculties properly. My awareness of my breasts issue is my footrule and guidelines for attaining **a quality life**.*

It is not a threat about my life, it's an urgency to plan for betterment. Another question that I would like to ask is, If you were diagnosed with Cancer of the breasts with stage III or IV and needed a chemotherapy or radiation, would you go for it? Me? Again my answer is: (there won't be a chemotherapy nor radiation.) That's why I have this book and that's my final answer.

I would like to focus not to myself nor the demands of the treatments but on how I can serve my GOD with full attention. I can't express enough these "deep inner thoughts and with the concept of death and overcoming fear," without contradicting the concept of others, I'm just being bold and honest enough to express everything in this whole book. Again, let me say it, we can celebrate our differences because we know that we are spiritual beings created in GOD's Image and share the common love and mercy of our powerful and mighty GOD.

I would like to emphasize that the most important part of our lives is the spiritual aspect of our very souls. We're created as spiritual beings and to develop spiritual energy, we have to cultivate a healthy connection with our Creator. The Bible repeatedly reveals that humans are created in GOD's Image. I would like to preserve the Image of GOD in me, here on earth and to the place we called HEAVEN.

I would like to close this book with a prayer I have in the beginning of this book.

MY INNER THOUGHTS PRAYER

O, my Almighty GOD, I bow down with humility, sincerely facing the reality of life, the life that I treasure so much, the life that You have entrusted in me.

Divine Creator, I can't thank You enough for this gift of life and all the blessings that I have received since birth. There are many things that I am thankful and grateful for, my LORD.

I am delighted to claim that I am created in Your Image and for being one of Your creations.

In You I entrusted back my life LORD, and I will wait until I receive Your final blessing, which is the beginning of eternity. I ask You LORD to grant me a safe journey when the time comes that You wanted me to be reunited with You and with my loved ones, to the place called HEAVEN and this I pray in the name of the Heavenly Father, Amen!

GOD BLESS THE READERS, THE SOUL BEINGS UNDERGOING TREATMENTS OF ANY SORT, THE CANCER SURVIVORS, THE DYING SOULS, THE WOMEN DISCERNING ON WHAT TO DO and TO ALL OF US LOVED BY OUR ALMIGHTY GOD.

ABOUT THE BOOK

This book is not about how to cope with grief nor about dwelling on it. It is about my own facing of the uncertainty of death. The uniqueness of this book is that, it is a confession of an ordinary woman like me. (actually this is my own confession) about pondering on how to face death gracefully and focusing on doing so, without valid reason such as suffering from terminal illness of any sort. It is indeed just plain boldness on my part. It is a challenge not to fear death, but a challenge to love death as a friend and to treat it as a blessing.

My goals in this book are: to express my inner thoughts and feelings, to share my concept of death to the readers, to let the world know that there is a healthy way, a healthy approach to death and utmost-ly to spend the time given to live a **"quality life"**.

Printed in the United States
By Bookmasters